Pentacle and the Occult

MARION PEARCE

GREEN MAGIC

Green Magic
Seed Factory
Aller
Langport
Somerset
TA10 0QN
England
www.greenmagicpublishing.com

Designed and typeset by Carrigboy, Wells, UK.
www.carrigboy.co.uk

ISBN 9781915580184

GREEN MAGIC

DEDICATION

This book is dedicated to Jon Randall, the Pentacle editor, whose hard work was essential in producing Pentacle.

I would also like to thank Tim Clay Ksc, who has helped me in producing the book.

The cover 'Hedge Rider II Huldra' is by Marc Potts

Marc Potts is a British artist and author from rural Devon.
The wooded valleys, wild moors and rugged coast play a part in
inspiring the feel of his art, along with a deep abiding
love of ancient Northern European history and its
folklore and mythology.

Marc has written two books,
"The Mythology of the Mermaid and Her Kin" (2000)
and "Ritual 1" (2018)

www.marcpottsart.com

Contents

CONTENTS

Alchemy – True and Moste Noble Arte

GARY NOTTINGHAM

Curiously, it has become common in our times for alchemy to be a "buzz word" for the more populist aspects of the magical arte, where people "pick 'n' mix as they will to suit their perceived spiritual needs of the moment. And yet, with respect to all those concerned with this approach and who write the articles and books on what they feel the alchemical arete to be, they are invariably wrong. Granted, many alchemical terms have been given the treatment and have been reinterpreted by the eminent psychologist Jung, but whatever their assumptions are, they are not alchemy.

Often you hear alchemy being associated with all manner of pseudo-magical concepts: the alchemy of "this" or the alchemy of "that," yet none of this is what was practiced by past masters of the art, such as Paracelsus, Sir George Ripley, the Cannon of Bridlington (1492), or by the good monk Basil Valentine, who penned the *Triumphal Chariot of Antimony*, a work that deals in some depth with the alchemical transmutation of antimony to produce all manner of wondrous substances, both magical and medicinal. Myself, I never understand how anyone can treat these ancient texts in any other way than what the authors are saying.

Of course, part of the problem is the language and imagery used; being deliberately obscure allows it to be open to all manner of ideas. But let me reassure the reader that what these adepts are portraying is an actual hands-on laboratory alchemical experience and not psycho-waffle. Often within these texts are signs and symbols to suggest the next part of the operation; for example, in the *Muter Libus* ("The Dumb Book"), which is an early alchemical text that uses pictures not words to instruct in the arte (hence the term Dumb Book), we can see a picture of a bull and a ram therein, which is telling the student to start "The Work" when the sun is in Aries or Taurus. The picture also emphasizes the full moon. This has an important contribution to make in any alchemical work as certain operations of the arte, which are performed at this time, will be critical to the success of the work.

Speaking of my own field of the arte spagyrics, which is the plant side of alchemy, also known as the "lesser work" – many of the techniques that are learnt and practiced with this discipline are of extreme importance to many alchemical operations, and it is therefore the usual starting point for any serious student of the arte.

Being an herbalist, I find a natural affinity for this aspect of the arte and therefore I will endeavour to explain some of its thinking. The whole alchemical arte can be summed up in the words "Solve et Coagula" – which is telling you to break down and rejoin together. These are the words inscribed on the Baphomet figure, wherein lies a mystery. There are three principles within the alchemical kingdom, and they are known as mercury, sulphur and salt. Whilst they are not their namesakes, they are often depicted as various figures or planetary icons.

MERCURY

This is the plant kingdom alcohol: ethanol, not any other alcohol. It carries the life force of the plant kingdom. It is best if it is fermented in situ and then distilled. By that, I mean that any plant that you are working with is fermented, and then the liquid is distilled seven times to get it dry and free of water. This distillation is referred to as "letting the eagle fly" or, in this case, seven eagles are flown. This method is slow, often called the "long path" and is considered the best as the mercury carries within it the plant signature that you are working with. The short way is simply to distil red wine or brandy; no other alcohol will do, as it is often shown as the White Woman or White Queen, sometimes called Diana or the Moon.

SULPHUR

The sulphur is the plant oils that are distilled, and it carries the soul of the plant and its personality. Some plants have more sulphur present than others; for example, rosemary and lavender will release large quantities of plant oils, whilst lemon balm has very little. This is the volatile sulphur, and it will combine easily with the mercury. There is also a fixed sulphur that can be obtained from the plant after it has been fermented. This dark water is then slowly evaporated, and then the thick tar that is produced is burned until it is reduced to a grey ash, from which a pure white salt can be produced. This burning process is called calcinations, or as the Old Texts say: "Vulcan turns all black things white" – which is a reference to this process. This is the sal sulphurous, the salt of the sulphur. The sulphur is shown as the sun, Apollo, the Red Man, or the Red King. Sometimes old texts will show a king swimming in the water, saying: "Save me, and you will win a great prize." This shows that the oils that have been distilled are now floating on top of the water and must be carefully gathered.

SALT

After the plant has had the mercury and the sulphur removed from it, it is then burned to a grey ash. From this ash, a fine white salt is produced, which is much prized. With this, alchemists will capture the "secret fire" that old texts often referred to. This fine white salt does take a little trouble to produce, and it must be made extremely clean and white before it can be used. This salt must be made pure, and it must be full of the secret fire that is then used to reanimate our matter, for then it is considered to be alchemical. The salt, which is the body of the plant that has been purified, will not mix with the mercury. If they are both placed in the same vessel, they will separate, and the alcohol will float on the top of the salts. This is important for some operations of the arte. It is the presence of the sulphur which will allow the mercury to enter the salt; that is, it is the soul that will bind the life force to the body.

It is the combining of these principles, be they plant, metal, or mineral, after they have been subjected to the alchemical arte which is the chemical wedding – a term that is often banded about with little or no knowledge of its real alchemical praxis. There are various ways that the alchemist will combine these principles, depending on what it is that they are endeavouring to produce. Simple tinctures can be produced full of the magical and medicinal properties of the plant, metal, or mineral that is required. Plants, metals and minerals will, if subjected to the arte aright, produce oils, mercury and salts, which can be combined accordingly. Sometimes plant salts are combined to produce a stone, a hard wax-like substance which has many properties relating to the plant, or elixirs, whereby the plant salts are made volatile and will fly upwards when in a glass retort, something that modern science says should not happen but will do if performed as the arte demands. This can produce highly effective medicines; although slow to produce, they are a pleasure to work with.

CIRCULATION

This is a term to describe an operation whereby a tincture or menstrum is placed in a large flask that has a specially designed flask placed on the top of it. This is then gently heated, which will allow the material to evaporate. As it does so, it will condense against the sides of the second flask and run back into the fluid in the bottom of the first flask. The process will often be started and finished according to lunar cycles and is a method of potentizing alchemical works. Frequently, alchemical workings will be governed by astrological timing and a work with a planetary energy will only be started at an auspicious time, so a good command of the astrologer's arte is a must. Others will combine their alchemical works with ritual magical practice and will further charge them with planetary energies. One magical group of my acquaintance has managed to produce various alchemical confections for each of the Sephira of the Tree of Life as aids when working with their energies. The alchemical arete is a rich field – more so if it is considered with those other disciplines of the Western Magical Tradition, astrology, Kabbalah and ritual magic – a fact that, on the whole, has not been appreciated.

Anahita – Ancient Persian Goddess and Zoroastrian Yazata

PAYAM NABARZ

The Indo-Iranian Anahita is an ancient Persian goddess who became a Zoroastrian Yazata (protective spirit or angel) and is still part of contemporary Zoroastrianism. Described as a beautiful maiden who is strong, tall and pure, she is depicted wearing a mantle embroidered with gold and holding the baresma (sacred plant) in her hand. She is the Goddess of all the Waters upon the Earth, her full title being *Aredvi Sura Anahita* which means moist, mighty and immaculate (pure), and she travels on her chariot pulled by four horses: Wind, Rain, Cloud and Sleet. Closely associated with the King's investiture, she is a goddess of sovereignty, thought by some to be the Persian Aphrodite, who also has some remarkable similarities to numerous other ancient goddesses, including Ishtar, Venus, Nana and Isis.

This is a review of some of the sources that mention Anahita, from ancient Persia to modern-day Iran, in chronological order to demonstrate a sense of the continuation of her influence. The review aims to set the scene for the more detailed academic papers and articles by various other authors in the Anahita anthology: *Anahita: Ancient Persian Goddess and Zoroastrian Yazata* (Editor Payam Nabarz, *Avalonia*, 2013).

Anahita is the mythical world river that emerges from Mount Hara into the great sea and is the source of all the waters. Anahita is also the planet Venus. It is within the Zoroastrian body of texts that much of her lore is preserved. She is one of the seven Zoroastrian Yazatas (protective spirits or angels). In the Zoroastrian hymn (Yasht) to her, we see a glimpse of her eminent pre-Zoroastrian role, as even Ahura Mazda pays her homage and asks for her help! There are some key Zoroastrian texts referring to Anahita: the *Aban Yasht 5, Yasna 65, and Aban Nyayis*. From the Zoroastrian text *Aban Yasht* (the hymn to angel-goddess Anahita), we have inherited a vivid description of her:

> *"… of all the waters upon the earth and the source of the cosmic ocean; you who drive a chariot pulled by four horses: Wind, Rain, Cloud, and Sleet; your symbol is the eight-rayed star. You are the source of life, purifying the seed of all males and the wombs of all females, also cleansing the milk in the breasts of all mothers. Your connection with life means warriors in battle prayed to you for survival and victory.*
>
> *A maid, fair of body, most strong, tall-formed, high-girded, pure … wearing a mantle fully embroidered with gold; ever-holding the baresma [sacred plant] in your hand … you wear square golden earrings on your ears … a golden necklace around your beautiful neck … Upon your head … a golden crown, with a hundred stars, with eight rays … with fillets streaming down."*[1]

The Persian Magi reciting the hymn to her had perhaps had their prayers answered in the form of visions. From the material we have, the visions might have appeared as the following: sitting on a beach or near a river; as midnight approaches and time slows, the sea parts, and a large silver throne appears; on either side of it sits a lion with eyes of blue flame. On the throne sits a Lady in silver and gold garments, proud and tall, an awe-inspiring warrior-woman, as terrifying as she is beautiful. Tall and statuesque she sits, her noble origins evident in her appearance,

---

1   From verses 126–128 of the *Aban Yasht* 5.

her haughty authority made clear and commanding through a pair of flashing eyes. A dove flies above her and a peacock walks before her. A crown of shining gold rings her royal temples; bejewelled with eight sunrays and one hundred stars, it holds her lustrous hair back from her beautiful face. Her marble-like white arms reflect moonlight and glisten with moisture. She is clothed with a garment made of thirty beaver skins, and it shines with the full sheen of silver and gold. The planet Venus shines brightly in the sky above her head.[2]

However, it is not just the Magi, Ahura Mazda or the 'good' people that make offerings to Anahita; the Daevas (demons) and the 'bad' people also make her offerings – she is worshipped by both sides. Indeed, in the *Aban Yasht,* warriors from opposing armies also make her offerings, but she only grants the 'good' warriors their prayers. This is attested to in Greek sources too, King Xerxes at dawn prayed for victory over the Greeks by pouring libations into the Hellespont, and flung a golden cup, a golden bowl, and a short sword into the sea.[3]

In addition to her warrior aspect, she is also a mother goddess:

> *"Who makes the seed of all males pure, who makes the womb of all females pure for bringing forth, who makes all females bring forth in safety, who puts milk into the breasts of all females in the right measure and the right quality."*[4]

Furthermore, she is associated with a number of different animals, and her totemic animals do vary as she changes in different parts of the Middle East and comes under the influence of different local customs and is exposed to varied cultures that span over a millennium. She is sometimes shown riding a lion

---

2 This description of Anahita is based on her description in Tony Allan, Charles Phillips and Michael Kerrigan, Myth and Mankind series: *Wise Lord of the Sky: Persian Myth* (London: Time Life Books, 1999), 32.

3 Jenny Rose, *Zoroastrianism: An Introduction* (I. B. Tauris, 2011), 53.

4 From verse 2 of the *Aban Yasht 5.*

when bestowing sovereignty to kings; e.g. there is a magnificent seal from the post-Achaemenid dynasties in Turkey that shows the king facing Anahita while she is standing on a lion surrounded by sun rays. In addition, the *De Natura Animalium,* by Aelian, refers to one of her shrines as containing tame lions, which would greet and wag their tails at visitors. On Sasanian ewer, we see her with doves and peacocks. This is further supported by recent discovery by Behzad Mahmoudi et al of a Sasanian stucco showing Anahita flanked by two winged lions and holding a dove.

The Sasanian stucco discovered in the Barz-eqawela in Lorestan provenance of Iran, by Behzad Mahmoudi et al from *Anahita: Ancient Persian Goddess and Zoroastrian Yazata.*

In the *Aban Yasht*, she rides in a chariot driven by four horses: the wind, the rain, the cloud, and the sleet. Indeed, this later vision of her is the theme of the famous pre-Raphaelite sculpture, *The Horses of Anahita*, and painting, *Anahita the Flight of Night*, by William Morris Hunt (1824–1879).

Anahita statue in snow, photo by Payam Nabarz.

The Horses of Anahita, by William Morris Hunt.[5]

---

5 *http://en.wikipedia.org/wiki/William_Morris_Hunt*

The sources referring to Anahita are not limited to Zoroastrian texts; there are also inscriptions left by kings; for example, circa 400 BCE, the Achaemenid king, Artaxerxes II Mnemon (404–359 BCE), inscribes in Ecbatana in his palace:

> "This hall [apadana] I built, by the grace of Ahuramazda, Anahita and Mithra. May Ahuramazda, Anahita and Mithra protect me against evil, and may they never destroy nor damage what I have built."[6]

Artaxerxes II, like other Achaemenid kings, was initiated by priests at a sanctuary of Anahita in Pasargadai during his coronation. Artaxerxes II built the temple of Anahita at Kangavar near Kermanshah, as well as many others. The Kangavar was a magnificent temple, four-fifths of a mile in circumference, built using cedar or cypress trees. All the columns and floor tiles were covered with gold and silver. It was perhaps one of the most breathtaking buildings ever built in the Middle East. Ancient kings were crowned by their queens in Anahita's temple in order to gain her protection and support. Anahita's blessing would bring fertility and abundance to the country.[7]

The pages of history turn, and eventually the Achaemenid Empire falls to 'Alexander the Accursed' but Anahita is carried into a new Greek-influenced empire.

Circa 200 BCE sees the dedication of a Seleucid temple in western Iran to "Anahita, as the Immaculate Virgin Mother of the Lord Mithra".[8] The blend of Greek and Persian cultures manifest themselves in the Seleucid dynasty.

---

6 *http://www.livius.org/aa-ac/achaemenians/A2Ha.html*

7 Official entry on Anahita by the Embassy of the Islamic Republic of Iran in Ottawa, Canada on their website: *http://www.salamiran.org/Women/ General/Women_And_Mythical_Deities.html*

8 *First Iranian Goddess of Productivity and Values* by Manouchehr Saadat Noury – Persian Journal, Jul 21, 2005. *http://www.iranian.ws/iran_news/publish/ printer_8378.shtml*

The Parthian Empire (circa 247 BCE–226 CE) replaces the Seleucid, and the Parthians expand the Anahita temple at Kangavar.

Mark Anthony marches in to Armenia (circa 37 BCE–34 BCE), and in one of the latter campaigns reached the Anahita temple at Erez:

> *"The temple of Erez was the wealthiest and the noblest in Armenia, according to Plutarch. During the expedition of Mark Antony in Armenia, the statue was broken to pieces by the Roman soldiers. Pliny the Elder gives us the following story about it: the Emperor Augustus, being invited to dinner by one of his generals, asked him if it were true that the wreckers of Anahit's statue had been punished by the wrathful goddess. 'No,' answered the general; 'on the contrary, I have today the good fortune of treating you with one part of the hip of that gold statue.' The Armenians erected a new golden statue of Anahita in Erez, which was worshipped before the time of St. Gregory the Illuminator."*[9]

The Sasanian Empire is formed circa 226 CE. The Temple of Anahita in Bishapur was built during the Sasanian era (241–635 CE). The temple is believed to have been built by some of the estimated 70,000 Roman soldiers and engineers who were captured by the Persian King Shapur I (241–272 CE), who also captured three Roman emperors: Gordian III, Phillip and Valerian. The design of the temple is noteworthy: water from the River Shapur is channelled into an underground canal to the temple and flows under and all around the temple, giving the impression of an island. The fire altar would have been in the middle of the temple, with the water flowing underground all around it. One might interpret this as a union of water–Anahita

---

9 *A History of Armenia* by Vahan M. Kurkjian, Bakuran. IndoEuropeanPublishing. com, 2008.

with fire–Mithra.[10] This fits well with Greek accounts of Persian reverence for fire and water. Indeed, Porphyry (circa 232–305 CE), in his work, *Cave of the Nymphs* (water spirits), states that the Persians worship in cave-like spaces:

> *"Thus also the Persians, mystically signifying the descent of the soul into the sublunary regions, and its regression from it, initiate the mystic (or him who is admitted to the arcane sacred rites) in a place which they denominate a cavern. For, as Eubulus says, Zoroaster was the first who consecrated in the neighbouring mountains of Persia a spontaneously produced cave, florid and having fountains, in honour of Mithra, the maker and father of all things; a cave, according to Zoroaster, bearing a resemblance of the world, which was fabricated by Mithra ... so to the world they dedicated caves and dens; as likewise to Nymphs, on account of the water which trickles, or is diffused in caverns, over which the Naiades, as we shall shortly observe, preside."*[11]

The line on water trickling reminds one of the Zoroastrian shrine of Pir-e Sabz, or Chek Chek ("drip drip" – the sound of water dripping), in the mountains of Yazd, Iran.

Eventually, the Sasanian Empire falls to the Arab Islamic invasion in 651 AD. Yet, even now Muslim pilgrims make their way to the 1,100 year-old shrine of Bibi Shahr Banoo, the Islamic female saint, near the old town of Rey (south of Tehran). The town of Rey is thought to be 5,000 years old, and the site of this shrine with its waterfall is believed by some to have once been an Anahita shrine and then become linked to later Islamic saints – a process seen frequently in Christianized Europe too; for example, sites sacred to the Celtic goddess Brighid became sites dedicated to Saint Brigit.

---

10 For the Temple of Anahita at Bishapur, see *http://www.vohuman.org/SlideShow/Anahita%20Bishapur/AnahitaBishapur00.htm*

11 On the Cave of the Nymphs in the Thirteenth Book of *The Odyssey* from the Greek of Porphyry, translated by Thomas Taylor, 1823.

Furthermore, according to Susan Gaviri's *Anahita in Iranian Mythology* (1993):

> "… it must not be forgotten that many of the famous fire temples in Iran were, in the beginning, Anahita temples. Examples of these fire temples are seen in some parts of Iran, especially in Yazad, where we find that after the Muslim victory these were converted to Mosques."[12]

Modern-day Zoroastrian pilgrims in Iran continue to visit the pre-Islamic Zoroastrian shrine of Pir-e Sabz, or Chek Chek ("drip drip" – the sound of water dripping), in the mountains of Yazd. This is still a functional temple and the holiest site for present-day Zoroastrians living in Iran, who take their annual pilgrimage to Pir-e Sabz Banu, "the Old Woman in the Mountain," also called Pir-e Sabz, "the Green Saint," at the beginning of summer. *Pir* means 'elder' and it can also mean 'fire'. The title of Pir also connotes a Sufi master. *Sabz* means 'green'.[13]

Commemorative gold coin with image of Anahita, 1997.

---

12 *Anahita in Iranian Mythology* (1993), 7. This book is written in Persian – translation here by Payam Nabarz.
13 For the temple at Pir-e Sabz, see *http://www.vohuman.org/SlideShow/Pir-e-Sabz/Pir-e-Sabz-1.htm*

Pilgrims also continue to visit Pir-e Banu Pars (Elder Lady of Persia) and Pir-e Naraki, located near Yazd. The Pir Banoo temple is in an area that has a number of valleys; the name of the place is Hapt Ador, which means 'Seven Fires'.[14]

The importance of Anahita in Armenia can further be seen in her images appearing in their current stamps and banknotes too.

A 5000 Dram banknote in Armenia with image of Anahita

---

14 For the temples of Pir e Banoo Pars and Pir e Naraki, see *http://www.sacredsites.com/middle_east/iran/zoroastrian.htm&http://www.heritageinstitute.com/zoroastrianism/worship/setinaraki.htm*

Animism

EMMA RESTALL ORR

There was a time, some years ago, when being able and willing to label oneself within the Pagan community seemed crucially important. Not only was it demanded of us that we declare our path to be Wicca, Heathenry, Druidry, and so on, but an array of adjectives was also needed: were we Gardnerian, Saxon, Brythonic, Feminist? Specificity was all. Those happy to call themselves simply Pagan were considered with suspicion as uncommitted, uninitiated, untrained.

No doubt such requirements still exist in certain quarters, but in the main it seems the tables have gently been turning. From where I stand, now a little on the edge, a great number appear keen to emphasise just how they are *not* aligned with any particular tradition: the path they are walking is proudly determined to be their own.

Empowered by such individuality, many express frustration at being categorised by labels. Others are frustrated at being associated with those who are using the same label but whose behaviour, they feel, is bringing that particular tradition into disrepute. Unable and unwilling to slide into the comfortable niche of a tradition, they are provoked into self-reflection, and begin, perhaps for the first time, to focus upon deconstructing the belief systems that underlie the various traditions. In doing so, many are exploring what it is that they actually believe.

In this process, a word I have been hearing a great deal more often of late is *animism*. Instead of Druid, or eco-Pagan, or hedge witch, for many an underlying belief in animism is considered a more accurate self-description. As a word that provides the metaphysical foundation of my own worldview, I have been acutely aware of it being discussed. Yet the discussions have left me wondering. For while, needless to say, I have met many Druids over the past 25 years whose religious practice, values and ethics are incompatible with my own, it was perhaps with a certain naiveté that I expected to find more common ground with others using the word *animist*. In fact, even though the word describes a belief and not a path, I have found almost as many fundamental differences between animists as I did between Druids. This stems from a crucial divergence in the basic definition.

SO WHAT IS ANIMISM?

English dictionaries tend to list animism as the attributing of spirit or soul to inanimate objects. I have always found such a definition to be quite gloriously damning in its evident self-contradiction. Most casual interpretations of the words *spirit* or *soul* suggest a force that allows for life, perhaps even sentience, consciousness, order or reason, and – given that *anima* is a Latin word for life or soul – to assert a belief that spirit or soul are present in inanimate objects, in *things*, is patently ridiculous.

Using this definition, then, animism is an erroneous belief. It is the mistake of the small child who assumes the wind-up toy is alive. It is the misunderstanding of the uncivilised man whose primitive life context has left him pitiably unable to distinguish body from soul, mind from matter. In other words, animism is a notion that, given a decent Western education, a reasonable person would and should leave behind.

To the animist, the comprehensively insulting nature of such an attitude can be wearying: it is a blunt instrument hitting the same spot again and again.

Given that I am a fully literate, well-educated, middle-aged Englishwoman, one might imagine such a critic would think twice about dismissing the foundational beliefs of my worldview as childish or primitive. Yet, it is still uncommon to encounter a member of conventional society who is willing to take animism seriously, and that can only provoke a thinking soul to consider more carefully the reasons why. Is it simply a continuing ignorance about what animism actually is?

Certainly, if we stay with the general definition above, animism is a distinct challenge to the predominant view within Western culture, primarily in that it disagrees as to what is, and what is not, a *thing*. Even without moving forward from the rather vague interpretations above, an entity that has a soul or spirit cannot be considered a mere thing. It is not existent in a perpetual state of passivity, and thus is evidently not just an object; like a human being, it is also a *subject*, a creature that experiences, that perceives, feels, communicates, considers, and must be treated as such.

Or have I now wandered clumsily into the territory not of soul or spirit but of mind, or consciousness? Does that make a difference? Thinkers in various fields, from the philosophical to the neurological, including the religious and the psychological, may have working definitions for some or each of these separate terms, but there is no agreement as to what they are, either within distinct disciplines or across their boundaries. Spirit and soul are very much spiritual jargon words, seldom now defined. And while we may be able to observe the mind, we do not understand how it is constituted. Consciousness is still a mystery; indeed, some dismiss it as an illusion, in just the same way as others over the past four or five centuries have dismissed the soul.

The bottom line, however, is this. Removing the last few self-contradictory words from the dictionary definition above, it is actually not that far removed from one that an animist may present himself as. Animism is the belief that there is a quality – whether we call it soul, spirit or mind – existent within (or integral to) what we understand to be matter. It is a quality that the non-animist does not accept to be there.

Yet surely, until we have an explicit understanding of just what this quality is, we have no definition of animism at all. And as long as we have no clear definition, perhaps animism will continue to be seen as an uneducated or childish perspective, a worldview drawn in fat wax crayons.

Allow me to address the issue from another tack.

Much Pagan spirituality, especially that influenced by religious traditions from overseas, teaches the value of transcending what is asserted to be the mental construct of dualism. We are guided *not* to perceive the world as good or bad, black or white, male or female, self or other, but instead encouraged to live without judging, to acknowledge the unique perspective of each individual as part of the colourful spectrum of existence, and all within the divine and essential wholeness of the universe.

One facet of dualism tenaciously persists, though: that of mind and matter. After more than a thousand years of European Christianity based on Plato's clear metaphysical divide, this appears to be the hardest to let go. Our language is thick with it, making it difficult to avoid the constant implication that there are two separate substances: the physicality of body and matter; and the ethereal nature of the experiencing or thinking self.

Such a view is common within Paganism too: the spirit or soul is often understood to be the coherent, conscious, communicating, sacred being, resident within the material form. Even where such ideas are not overt, they are revealed in attitudes towards death, when the spirit or soul is thought to be released, flying free of its mortal bodily anchor to journey to other planes, other worlds, or other lives.

For some adherents of animism, their worldview is implicitly dualistic too. The spirit of a river or a tree is envisioned as a misty, ethereal coherence that dwells within the flowing water or the wood and sap of the tree. Like a human ancestor, it is a consciousness with whom the Pagan seer can communicate, a being that requires respect and fair exchange. For some, that spirit is immortal, surviving the felling of the tree or the draining of the river, in the same way that the spirit is believed to survive the death of a human ancestor.

It is in this respect that, I feel, the fundamental divergence exists within animism: between the dualists and those for whom dualism is not convincing. I step forward as one of the latter. Like many thinkers over the past two and a half thousand years, I cannot overcome the principal philosophical flaw of dualism: that if mind and matter were indeed made of two distinct kinds of stuff, there would be no possibility of a communicating connection.

As such, I am aware of being judged by some as unspiritual, even blasphemous in my attitude. I am often reminded of a Pagan conference at Fairfield Halls, Croydon, many years ago when I hollered from the main stage that the moon is "just a f—king rock in the sky." If I am unwilling to acknowledge that the sacred quality of the moon is its eternal, perhaps even separable, soul, it is assumed I do not hold it as divine. For the only other option in our Western culture is deemed to be the opposing belief that is materialism or physicalism, where nothing exists but dull, mundane matter.

Neither, however, am I a materialist, even where the perspective is enriched as a naturalistic panpsychism. Philosophically, that route raises problems that I feel to be just as profound. Although the cutting edge of scientific exploration only emphasises how little we know of matter, it is still fundamentally, categorically, different from mind: matter has no inner reality. Indeed, it could be said (and has been said by some of the greatest minds of our heritage) that we know more of mind, or of the inner experience of thinking, than we do about anything that lies beyond that thinking, including matter.

Perhaps some will feel that I am asking too much, objecting to my desire to understand what is an unknowable quality, a divine essence of life, of universal becoming. Indeed, that I am asking the question at all may feel terribly secular, and certainly far more philosophical than spiritual. After all, the interface between body and soul may well be crystal clear to a deity (to God, gods, or some sacred unity) and may ever remain beyond our human potential for comprehension.

However, my need to question is inherent. Nor do I believe it simply to be a mental fidget: there are consequences to sloppy thinking, not just to those judging animism from outside its beliefs, but also to those apparently holding such beliefs.

For example, if some aspects or parts of nature are subjects able to perceive and experience, which are they? Equally, are there parts of nature that cannot? Is it possible to draw a line? It may be blurred, but many animists do draw that line, whether consciously or subconsciously: a desert has a spirit, a mind, but perhaps a grain of sand does not. Although many would say that a river is awake, what of a raindrop or a bowl of water, of the hydrogen and oxygen atoms within it, the quarks and neutrinos? What of bones and books, what of leather and oil? That which has no capacity for perception, for experience or memory, is a *thing*, and a thing can be used without care or consideration.

I reject the possibility of there being a line.

There are further vital questions. For example, if some being has spirit, is the animist asserting that it is aware, or self-aware? Can it think, feel, remember, abstract or consider? Are some parts of nature *more* conscious than others? And given that we cannot know nature except through the filters of our own perceiving minds, on what basis could we assert the answer to any of the above?

Furthermore, where we believe there is soul, experience or sentience, does it extend beyond the core of the body? Does an ocean feel not only its depths and breaking waves, but its riverine limbs and its well springs? Does a tree experience touch and communicate through the microorganisms in and around its roots? Does a stone remember its millions of years of existence? With its long experience so utterly different from that of a human being, what could the interaction between us be? What wisdom could be imparted, what harm could be caused?

The animist seeker sits beneath a tree, striving to listen or to communicate, and the sceptic laughs at what he judges to be anthropomorphic egocentrism, the projection of human-style consciousness onto a non-human world. I would say that such scepticism is based on an erroneous assumption, for to assume that all within nature experiences existence in the same way that a human does is clearly ridiculous. But is the seeker also making an error? What could non-human consciousness look like?

Were we to understand, or even simply to define, just what this quality is which the animist perceives within nature, perhaps we would be closer to answering such questions.

Before I wrote *The Wakeful World*, I could offer a pretty coherent and concise definition of animism. Perhaps in five year's time, when my mind is busy deconstructing another aspect of human reality, I shall be able to do so again. The impetus for writing the book, however, came from the critical need to clarify for myself just what is meant by that magical quality the animist perceives, so broadly existent within nature.

It is not a book of fact. But my hope is that it offers a possible answer to the concerns and questions I have raised in this article. As a result, it is a rich book, one that needs chewing and pondering. Exploring dualism and materialism as a means of introduction, I journey towards a definition of animism that has within it an understanding of that *animating* quality. Recognising that there is no certainty within the realms of metaphysics, I hope too that my words provoke thought in each reader, encouraging them to consider of what they themselves believe nature, body and mind are made.

All beliefs have implications, and the decision to turn a crayon sketch into a precision drawing is an important act for me. Animism is perhaps the most radically challenging worldview within our current Western world. It is a profoundly dangerous idea to present to this unsustainable and inequitable capitalist, consumerist culture, so entirely based upon the exploitation of nature. If, after all, we perceive nature as the integration of countless experiencing, feeling, remembering, communicating beings then our ethical base and thus our behaviour cannot help but change.

Emma Restall Orr's book is *The Wakeful World: Animism, Mind and the Self in Nature* (Moon Books). For more information on this and her previous books, go to her website *http://emmarestallorr. org*

Austin Osman Spare – The Nescient Father of Chaos

JAQ D. HAWKINS

Modern chaos magic is often connected with the magical methods of Austin Osman Spare, yet Austin Spare died twenty years before the advent of this area of magic. His methods served as inspiration to the first chaos magicians of the 1970's, although other elements were essential to the formulation of the new discipline, many of which were never known by Spare.

Austin Osman Spare's art and magic were very closely intertwined in his life. Spare came from humble roots, yet when the young Spare showed an unusual aptitude for drawing, the family managed to find the funds to send him to art school. At the age of 13, he left school to serve an apprenticeship in a stained-glass works, but continued his education at art college in Lambeth (South London) in the evenings. During this time, he won a scholarship to the Royal College of Art and began serious artistic study.

Spare very quickly gained popularity in the art world. He exhibited his first picture in 1904, at the age of 17, in the Royal Academy. Then, in 1905, he published his first book, *Earth Inferno*. It was primarily meant to be a book of drawings but included commentaries that showed some of his insight into the workings of the human mind and his spiritual leanings.

Spare's drawings, often depicting human figures in grotesque postures or semi-human spirit forms, were uniquely expressive, as were his writings on magic and art. Spare continually tells us that we have the ability to think for ourselves – a seemingly simple statement, yet a concept that is very difficult for a large percentage of our conformist society to truly grasp. In the last three decades, since his work has become well-known among modern magicians, there has been a massive increase in the numbers of people who try to imitate Spare's methods and yet miss the point of his primary message that we must each of us develop our own methods of magic, or else we are but pale imitators.

The word 'chaos' first appears in connection with Spare in his first book, *Earth Inferno*. The title of the first full-page drawing is: "DESTINY, HUMANITY, and THE CHAOS OF CREATION." The word Chaos here might be interpreted equally as creation or disorder, and it is up to the readers of Spare's works to decide which is most appropriate to the pictures that he includes, as well as the idea he attempts to convey.

It is also in *Earth Inferno* that Spare first refers to Kia, which is Spare's symbol for the cosmic self, which uses Zos (his identification for himself as body, mind and soul in connection with sorcery) as its field of activity. Another drawing in *Earth Inferno* is titled simply, CHAOS. It faces a page that contains quotes from *Dante's Inferno*, and from *The Book of Revelation*, as well as his own caption:

"The perpetual youth of man arises, draws aside the curtain-Faith (a token of humanity's LIMITED knowledge), and exposes the inferno of THE NORMAL."

Above the drawing itself, which depicts a man drawing aside a curtain to see a mass of human bodies writhing together in various postures, is the entreaty:

"Oh! Come with me, the KIA and the ZOS, to witness this extravagance."

Opening the book to these two pages exposes the reader to an insight of the human drama, as only a philosopher can step aside and look upon it. Spare refers elsewhere in the book to "Creating a CHAOS of reflection." Spare's drawings and commentaries on youth and blindness unmasked throughout this book leave plenty of room for reflection within interpretation through the mind of each reader.

During the time that this book was first published, the young Spare was residing with a novelist, the Reverend Robert Hugh Benson. One of the more unusual stories one often hears about Spare's magical conjurings occurred while Spare was on a walk with Benson. It was a clear summer day and, as a joke, Benson suggested that Spare try some rainmaking. Spare, always willing to oblige, drew a sigil on a scrap of paper and concentrated his will upon it. Within a few minutes, a cloud formed overhead and drenched them both.

There are several stories about Spare's ability to achieve instant results with this sort of magic; most of the stories about Spare appear in *Images and Oracles of Austin Osman Spare*, by Kenneth Grant (Frederick Muller Ltd., London, 1975), who knew Spare for many of his later years.

In 1908, Spare held an art exhibition at Bruton Gallery. By this time, he had become very popular among the "smart set" in London – the art collectors and dandies of the time. About 1910, he joined Aleister Crowley's Argentium Astrum, an occult order of a similar nature to the Golden Dawn. This association did not last long. Spare had begun work on his most well-known book, *The Book of Pleasure*, and had his own ideas concerning the practice of magic.

This book was first published in 1913, but is more easily found today in reprint editions, most often limited to 500 or 1000 copies. It is considered his most important magical work and includes detailed instructions for his system of sigilization and the well-known "death postures". Some of the drawings in this book are more detailed than previously published works. The writing goes into deeper detail of Spare's philosophy as well. He has much to say here about human hypocrisy, outward show of religion and even some magical groups and the meanings of true personal freedom and power. It is also in this book that Spare describes his "NeitherNeither" principle and that of "free belief".

These concepts are important keys to magic – and ones that should be read in their original form to be fully appreciated. This is where many students of magic find that they must shift their thinking processes if they are to find value in what may appear to some as bizarre ramblings. In fact, every word and sentence of this particular book is an alchemist's goldmine of the "secrets" of magic that many spend lifetimes trying to discover, yet the meanings are clear only to those who have already achieved a similar mindset to that which Spare tries to describe within those pages.

In 1916, Spare joined the army and served as an official war artist during the First World War. He was posted to Egypt, which had a great effect on him. The animal-headed gods and magical religion of ancient Egypt could hardly fail to appeal to the insightful nature of the artist and mystic.

During the Second World War, Spare suffered an injury when his home in London was devastated by a bomb-blast, which paralyzed his right side. Naturally, this caused him a great deal of depression, as he believed for some time that he would never draw again. However, within six months time, he had recovered the use of his right arm and began to learn to draw all over again.

This incident is related in detail in the book, *Images and Oracles of Austin Osman Spare*. Grant credits Spare's personal elementals and familiars for the speed of his recovery. He also points out that Spare's memory was affected by the blast, and that many of the drawings done during this recovery period were dated many years earlier.

In 1921, Spare published *The Focus of Life*, which is another book of drawings that includes his unique and magical commentaries. The word "chaos" comes in again here in relation to the normality of chaos in the natural order of things and in self, "The more chaotic – the more complete I am." Spare speaks mostly to himself as Zos in this book. He has become the confident philosopher and has much to say to us, if we are able to listen. He speaks here of existence, of sex, of ecstasy and sensation. Spare seems to continue many of the ideas from *The Book of Pleasure* here, about self-love, belief and the "chaos of the normal."

From 1921 to 1924, he was at the height of his artistic success; then, in 1924, the outward successes of his artistic career conflicting with the philosopher within brought him to a turning point. Spare had become disenchanted with the trendy artistic friends and benefactors with whom he had been so popular. He wrote another book titled *The Anathema of Zos*, in which he effectively excommunicated himself from these people, flaunting their hypocrisies in their faces.

He returned to South London and obscurity to find the freedom to develop his philosophy, art and magic. There is little known about the activities of Spare during this time. He lived in a small basement apartment, caring little for money or fame. He made his living drawing portraits of the common people in his local pub and selling them for small amounts of money. He was offered larger sums on occasion but refused to accept them.

Although he wasn't publishing during this time, Spare continued to write. In 1947, Spare met Kenneth Grant and became more involved with other occultists of the time. From 1948 to 1956, he began work on a definitive grimoire of the Zos Kia Cultus, which is referred to in his various writings. This is unfinished and is being synthesized from Spare's papers by Kenneth Grant, who inherited Spare's papers.

Austin Osman Spare died in May of 1956. Most of his unpublished papers went into the hands of Kenneth Grant, who has published much of the material in *Images and Oracles of Austin Osman Spare*, but there remains some unpublished material which Grant intends to publish when time from his Typhonian series allows.

More recently, in 1992, Fulgar Press, London, released a limited edition of texts and drawings apparently composed by Spare during the early 1950's. The title is *Axiomata and the Witches Sabbath*. The combined texts are printed back-to-back. Included is a preface written by Robert Ansell, who is known to have collected and published bookplates drawn by Spare.

Collectors of Spare's works have had varying comments to make about the written text of these books, but all agree that there is quite a difference from his earlier works. The nature of this difference I leave to readers of these works to decide for themselves.

After his death, Spare's published works did not entirely disappear, but became collector's items among a few magicians in the U.K. The material began to resurface in the early 1970's in small occult magazines.

In issue #4 of a magazine called *Agape*, a magician by the name of Lionel Snell published a facsimile of *The Anathema of Zos* along with an essay titled *Spare Parts*, which was a commentary on *The Book of Pleasure*. This essay is reproduced in a collection of articles by and about Spare called *Excess Spare*, which was recently available from a non-profit group known as Thee Temple Ov Psychick Youth, or T.O.P.Y. It also appears in another collection of Spare's works titled *The Collected Works of Austin Osman Spare*, which was edited and compiled by Christopher Bray. This was published by Bray's own publishing company, The Sorcerer's Apprentice Press (Leeds, 1986, second revised edition), in limited editions. This volume contains all of Spare's previously published books except *The Book of Satyrs*, as well as a very interesting introduction by Christopher Bray, and the Lionel Snell essay already mentioned. Reprints of Spare's writings surface periodically in a number of forms. Lionel Snell published a book in 1974 titled *SSOTBME* (Nigel Grey Turner, Surrey, 1979), which reflects the idea of the world being shaped by our perception of it, and other ideas common to much of Spare's writings and modern chaoist philosophy.

It is very likely that the publishing of this material contributed to the interest in Spare by today's academic magicians of various persuasions. That Spare's material and the books written by Snell influenced the magicians who were to form the Illuminates of Thanateros, or IOT, a few years later is commonly known. The word 'Thanateros' is a conjunction made from the Greek 'Thanatos' which means death, and "Eros" which means sex. The word can also mean 'poison'.

Those familiar with magical symbolism will recognize the significance in these meanings. Death (the destruction principle) and sex (the re-creative principle) are very basic concepts in magic. It is the symbolic tearing down of the old to make room for the new, as the Phoenix who is destroyed in flame yet rises made anew from the ashes.

The relationship between the concepts of procreation and death was a strong element in the writings of Austin Osman Spare. Poison, for all its sinister reputation, is akin to medicine, as any doctor or herbalist knows.

The most powerful healing drugs include ingredients which are poisonous by themselves, in quantities that will kill the disease without destroying the host. In magic, it is necessary to destroy the disease of preconceived beliefs in order for the soul to be free to perform.

A societal bifurcation, The Illuminates of Thanateros, began in the late 1970's in England. A young Englishman by the name of Peter J. Carroll was living in an area of South East London called Deptford, best known for the press gangs (who recruited for the Royal Navy by knocking unsuspecting strangers over the head, after which they awoke on a ship at sea) and for being the area where the punk fashion originally took root in London.

For all its rough edges, this area attracted an interesting collection of artists and intellectuals, many of whom were involved in various aspects of the 1960's revival of magic and interest in new forms of music and philosophy.

Most of the focus of magic in England at that time was either on the Wiccan traditions, with all of their religious overtones, or on Thelemic Ceremonial Magick and the very traditional organizations that are associated with it. Mr. Carroll was one of those who had more eclectic ideas about magic in general at that time and was familiar with the writings of Austin Osman Spare.

Carroll was a regular contributor to a magazine called *The New Equinox*, which was edited and published by another creative young Englishman named Ray Sherwin. Mr. Sherwin and Mr. Carroll became acquainted and there were frequent visits between them. At first, this was in London, where it was not uncommon for a group of magicians to gather for social occasions at a block of flats in Deptford known as Speedwell House.

It is difficult to pinpoint an exact moment when Chaos Magic of the IOT flavour began, but one significant occasion was the 'Deptford Olympics Goat Roast' which coincided with the Montreal Olympics in 1976. This was, as the title suggests, a sports day held on a waste ground behind Speedwell House, followed by a grand barbeque party complete with spitted goat, live punk ensemble and a pyrotechnic display provided by some of the local anarchists.

Peter Carroll was working on a magical treatise titled *Liber MMM* during this period, which was later published by Ray Sherwin as *Liber Null*. After a trip to the East, Carroll spent some time living in Yorkshire where he spent a fair amount of time in the company of Mr. Sherwin who had written and published a few books of his own, including the underground classics *Theatre of Magick* and *The Book of Results*. *The Book of Results* was re-issued by Revelations 23 Press, Sheffield, in 1992.

Sherwin and Carroll had many a conversation on the subject of magical theory and the situation of magical groups in England. They shared a dislike for hierarchical organizations, which led to discussions on the plausibility of a non-hierarchical magical Order. At some point during this time, the two of them became the original IOT. Carroll had suggested the name, which he may have had in mind while working on his earlier writings. It was during this time in Yorkshire that he wrote *Psychonaut*, which was later published in the same volume as *Liber Null* by Samuel Weiser, Inc.

An ad was placed in *The New Equinox* to recruit members, and the group began to take form. One very noteworthy point about the early members of the IOT is that they were mostly university educated. Peter Carroll had been a chemistry major and Ray Sherwin studied theology and has taught English at Cairo University. Another of the early members, Charles Brewster, was a geology major who subsequently wound up as an instrument technician working for the research group at University College, whose photon detector identified the first 'black hole'.

During this same time period, unknown to these bright young magicians, a man by the name of Mandelbrot was developing chaos mathematics at the IBM Research Center in Yorktown Heights, New York.

The melding of chaos math and science, and Chaos Magic, was still to come. It would be Peter Carroll who would first notice the relationships between the two. *The New Equinox* advertisement appeared in 1977. The issue also contained an editorial rant written by Ray Sherwin encouraging academic magicians to get on with magic and get some results, rather than spending their time pondering "which way up their pentacles should be." This was a reference to the inevitable bickering among different factions of occultists which occurs still today.

Part of the idea of modern Chaos Magic is that all methods are correct, one tradition as valid as another, so long as it gets results. The IOT was described in the ad as "readying itself to spread the gnosis," the methods described as "not dependent on any symbolic system or mystification … they are the root techniques powering all systems." The advertisement also went on to say that the IOT was not an artificial hierarchy, which is one of the main points that separates the lOT from other magical Orders. The intention was that degrees would indicate attainment rather than authority, and that leaders and authority figures would not exist beyond the bare minimum needed to organize things.

Liber Null was drawing more attention than the ad itself at this time and, human nature being what it is, the ideal of non-hierarchy was already somewhat compromised by the inclination of people to see Peter Carroll as the leading figure in the IOT. There were some experiments in collective work with this early group, but it was not long before Ray Sherwin dropped out of the IOT and Peter Carroll went on to officially form 'The Pact of the Illuminates of Thanateros,' or simply 'The Pact'. Sherwin and Carroll remained friends and Sherwin is still involved in Chaos Magic in England, although not directly with the IOT.

In the early 1980's, a copy of *Liber Null* appeared in Germany. There was no copyright or address for the author, so a magician and writer (known to the public today as Frater U.D.) translated it into the German language. Frater U.D. was a teacher of practical magick, and it was inevitable that he and Peter Carroll would meet. Frater U.D. was initiated into The Pact and given a grade appropriate to his experience. He celebrated his first Chaos-Mass with Carroll in 1985.

This was only the beginning of the proliferation of the IOT. In the mid-1980's, The Pact had become an international organization, including temples in England, Germany, Austria, Switzerland and Australia. An annual meeting at a castle in Austria became a traditional setting for the international factions to gather together and share ideas about magic, which continues to this day.

The magazine *Chaos International* appeared in 1986 and became associated with the IOT, although articles and opinions were certainly not limited to Pact members. The original idea of this magazine was that editorship would change with each issue and that the magazine would represent all Chaos Magicians and groups following this current. The first two issues were edited by P.D. Brown and Ray Sherwin, then the editorship passed through the hands of a few others before settling in the capable hands of Ian Read, who has done an excellent job with it ever since. Other magazines focusing on the subject of the chaos current have come and gone, but *Chaos International* has continued on and its popularity has spread to other countries. Part of the reason for this is the lack of bias for particular ideas – although the magazine is still associated with The Pact, it still represents the freedom of thought and ideas indicative of all Chaos Magicians.

In 1988, it was decided that Lola Babalon (a European member who had been living in California for two years) would start an IOT temple in the U.S.A. She had studied magic with Frater U.D. and had attained the 3rd degree required to start a temple. This temple was eventually dissolved when Lola resigned from the IOT for personal reasons, and other temples in Southern California now represent the American faction of the IOT. Lola has remained active in the magical community and is involved with another new magical group in Southern California.

In an announcement in *Chaos International #12*, Peter Carroll announced his formal retirement as the head of the IOT. Carroll stated that he had decided to spend more time with his family and on his business. He also states that he leaves the organization in good hands, although he does not name his successor. One may speculate that this is because the occult climate in England had been a bit strained at the time, due to the pirating and showing of a film with reported occult overtones on British television which had given fuel to the fire of religious fanaticism against all people and organizations related to any form of New Age or occult activity, but I must emphasize that this is only speculation. He mentions that he may continue to write "articles and the occasional book."

The history of the IOT looked at as a whole is fascinating. The organization is modern, yet quite serious. The rapid spread of IOT temples to several countries and its endurance indicate not only an appeal to contemporary magic users, but also a synchronicity with the times in which it has grown up. There are other groups and individuals who practice some form of Chaos Magic, yet the IOT has become so well-known as to be looked upon as a central (dis)organizational force. History will likely show its importance along with other well-known magical organizations, but with a special emphasis on revolutionary ideas and open-mindedness for new methods and ideas uncommon to magical groups in the past. It will be interesting to observe the unfolding of this history as it continues into the coming years.

In some areas, new Chaos groups have been formed by ex-IOT members who have left the Order for whatever reasons. This is especially prevalent in America where the cultural influences are not as conducive to the original non-hierarchical intent of the founders of the Order. One could almost visualize the spreading of Chaos in a fractal pattern of self-similarity through the proliferation of these splinter groups.

Chaos is also making itself apparent in the workings of other academic magical groups. The writings of A.O. Spare, Kenneth Grant, Ray Sherwin, Ramsey Dukes, Peter Carroll, and others of recent popularity have become basic textbook information among ceremonial magicians – just as the writings of Dion Fortune, the Farrars, and others are classics to the Wiccan communities.

Articles relating to Chaos Magic appear with increasing frequency in mainstream New Age magazines. There are still only a few books on the market dealing directly with Chaos, partially because good books on the subject are still often privately published in limited editions.

Chaos Magic is a return to basic magical principles, yet it is seen as an advanced level of magical knowledge because one must learn about all the trappings of illusion and deception in 'systems' of magic before the basics can be seen for what they are.

In ritual we 'deceive' ourselves into a belief which can then become reality. A.O. Spare had much to say about the role which belief, or suspension of it, plays in ritual. The art of looking beyond what we simply accept as true to alternate possibilities plays a part in science as well as magic.

Many of the basic principles of how things work in magic are beginning to find some explanations in an area of science which has only recently begun to gain respectability. It has been very appropriately dubbed, 'chaos science'. Chaos science is an area still not entirely accepted by mainstream science, yet it is something which is not likely to go away, despite the discomfort it creates for the status quo. There are several good books in print on the subject of chaos science, yet these are written by scientists who invariably explain the subject in their own familiar terms, which those of us who did not major in physics or mathematics may have a little trouble keeping up with.

It is my purpose in this article to explain the various elements of chaos science – including just a little history – to the average reasonably intelligent person who is not familiar with the language of scientists and may even shy away from physics or math. The need for this became apparent to me some time ago when I first began investigating the subject myself. There were a lot of people who asked me to explain this subject to them, despite the fact that I make no secret of the fact that I lack a science degree myself.

The last straw was when a friend of mine (who is a well-educated, published writer and who teaches Latin and Greek) came to me for an explanation, admitting to being bewildered by the same books that I use for reference. If the reader holds a science or mathematics degree, and is looking for detailed information on this subject or instructions for programming a computer to draw fractal patterns, I recommend that they refer to one of the books written solely on the chosen area and leave this chapter to us common folk.

THE MEANING OF CHAOS:

Many creation myths begin with a point called chaos, from whence comes all matter. Chaos can be represented as a calm centre of non-creation or as a tumultuous ocean of possibilities, but the concept of being the beginning and end of all things is almost universal among the known mythologies of the world.

The chaos scientists are attempting, among other things, to explain the nature of creation from infinite potential in their studies on the workings of nature. It is an area where mathematicians, physicists, biologists, chemists, and even meteorologists have had to learn to communicate with one another in order to recognize the similarity of the natural laws governing the behaviour of a wide variety of systems in the real world. In their own scientific way, they look for a cause for things where apparently acausal effects have occurred.

Chaos science studies the connections between different types of irregularity in our world. It tackles the problem of the nature of disorder, which scientists have habitually avoided for many years. It seems likely that eventually they will be able to explain it all to us in great detail and become respected among their peers for all their trouble but, for now, the science is still considered new and somewhat suspect. Even the generally accepted sciences of psychology and hypnosis are still considered somewhat dubious in some quarters. New areas of science have traditionally gone through a period of resistance before being slowly accepted into the mainstream of established theory. Chaos theory will come into its own in time.

Chaos science is largely a study of self-similar patterns in nature and natural phenomena. These patterns – often referred to as "chaotic" or "random" – include studies of such areas as the cause of turbulence in fluids, the patterns of coastlines or cloud formations, cyclic patterns in such things as the rise and fall of species populations and the self-similar patterns of the growth of living things. All of these things fall under the heading of chaos science. Certain terms and phrases have become part of the language of chaos science. Among them are: the butterfly effect, fractals, strange attractor and the Mandelbrot set.

It is becoming clear through the study of irregularity and unpredictability that in the real world, the laws of order and chaos are intertwined, each giving rise to the other. The strange laws behind chaotic phenomena hold explanations for the things that we find remarkable in our world, from such physical oddities as the pattern of the human heartbeat, the irregularity of a coastline and the path of a forest fire, to the nature of creative thought in the human mind, and even creation itself.

It has been observed that very ordered systems will fall apart in nature, such as the human heartbeat, which is naturally aperiodic. On the other hand, apparently chaotic systems will give rise to order.

Scientific reductionism imagines that everything in nature can be disassembled and reassembled into component parts, such as molecules, atoms, electrons, etc., and that at some point we could discover the very smallest of basic particles which would allow us to understand all that there is to know about the universe and everything in it.

The reductionists of the nineteenth century dismissed chaotic systems as randomness, or as passive entropy, which is a term referring to the progressive disorganization of useful energy in a system. Any machine in operation turns some of the energy into a form which cannot be recovered and used again, therefore requiring an energy source to fuel it. This was maddening to the nineteenth century scientists who theorized that through Newtonian laws, it should be possible to invent a perpetual motion machine.

This is a demonstration of a dissipative structure. Dissipation suggests something which falls apart, as opposed to structure. A dissipative structure is a system which is capable of maintaining its identity only if it remains open to the flux and flow of its environment. It is a creature of a non-linear world, which is an area which didn't attract very much scientific interest at the time. To understand what constitutes the scientific study of chaos, it is helpful to explain the meanings of some of the terms and phrases which have become part of the language of chaos.

The Butterfly Effect: "The butterfly effect" is a name given to a phenomenon which is more technically referred to as "sensitive dependence on initial conditions." This idea was first modelled on a computer graph by Edward Lorenz, an MIT meteorologist who had a fascination for the way patterns in the atmosphere changed over time, keeping within statistical averages yet never exactly repeating themselves – the butterfly effect.

A standard weather forecast chart or any similar prediction chart can approximate a result from initial conditions, but a minute fluctuation in data can have dramatic effects.

In 1960, he had been working on feeding non-linear equations into a computer to try to model the Earth's atmosphere. He repeated a weather forecast, rounding off the figures in the equations to three decimal places, rather than the six decimal places used in the first run. A scientist would expect to find similar results from the two tests, with only a slight variation caused by the tiny inaccuracy. What actually appeared on the graphs resulting from this test was a shocking revelation. At first, the typical graphic pattern of rises and dips above a central line followed a similar pattern, with the expected slight variation for inaccuracy, then suddenly the pattern split into two entirely different patterns, completely unrelated to one another. The combination of nonlinearity and iteration had magnified the microscopic difference in the equations in the two computer runs, indicating that a very slight variable in the initial conditions of the test resulted in an entirely different outcome. This was compared within the context of weather patterns to the example of the microscopic effects of a butterfly flapping its wings in Hong Kong, which could set up a change in air currents, magnified progressively through currents in the atmosphere until it resulted in a rainstorm in New York. Thus the term, "butterfly effect". In a non-linear equation used to model a system in nature, a very small variable can have an extreme effect.

An evolving system which has remained constant for a large range of values can suddenly reach a critical point, where the values split up (referred to as a bifurcation) and the system jumps into an entirely different behaviour, such as turbulence. In the area of natural law, scientists have allowed themselves to believe that given an approximate knowledge of a system's initial conditions, such as a weather pattern or the flow of lava from a volcano, they can calculate the approximate behaviour of the system. Yet these systems can frustrate the researchers by behaving erratically, suddenly moving in a direction completely out of sequence with the predictions.

The study of newly recognized laws for these sudden variations in the behaviour of natural phenomena is a major factor in what is now called chaos science. It has been shown that natural systems follow patterns with certain parameters, but with disturbances. There is an order within disorder in nature, which has only recently (through the studies of Lorenz and a handful of other scientists) been possible to model with computers. What was previously believed to be just random behaviour in natural systems is now shown to be subject to a different set of natural laws than the classical Newtonian laws of deterministic science. This different set of natural laws applies universally to a wide spectrum of different types of irregularity, from biological systems to geological formations and even economical patterns. The universality of these laws is the study of chaos science.

Blood from a Stone – Alchemical Processes in the 0=0

"The alchemical process is a method for self-knowledge that the soul undergoes far outside its realm of existence."

– Mary Anne Atwood.

IN THE BEGINNING

The neophyte 0=0 ritual is a summary of the candidate's work in the entire Outer Order. The ritual can be looked at in many ways on different levels, including the viewpoint of spiritual alchemy. There is a certain amount of disagreement amongst alchemists and alchemical texts about how many stages and in what order these processes occur. The most popular and earlier version seems to be based on four stages, commencing with the Nigredo (blackening), followed by the Albedo (whitening), Citrinitas (yellowing) and the final stage, Rubedo (reddening). Whether by accident or design, these seem to be a fitting arrangement for the 0=0 ritual.

NIGREDO

The candidate starts off in the Nigredo (melanosis) state, hoodwinked, for the Mother of Darkness has blinded them with her hair and the Father of Darkness has hidden them under his wings. The candidate's soul is in a post-fall state, the stone that has been rejected, the unrefined *prima materia*. As such, the candidate is in a state of putrefaction and in need of earthly purification and consecration to help him with his journey through the underworld to his personal realisation of divinity and its individualisation.

The Keryx opens the door to admit the candidate. As holder of the Caduceus, the tool of Hermes, he is the mercurial force acting on the candidate's unrefined state and is instrumental in the first stage of their personal transmutation.

Alchemically speaking, this stage is about putrefaction, death and decay. In old alchemical texts, this phase was often represented by a bird, usually a raven or a crow, descending into darkness. Psychologically speaking, it has been compared to a dark night of the soul – a confrontation with Jung's idea of the shadow self. This process is associated with the transformative planet Saturn and could explain why the neophyte grade is opened utilising knocks in the order given by the planetary square of Saturn if it were laid over the $0=0$ temple floor plan.

In keeping with the morbid undertones of this stage, decapitation is also associated with it and symbolises the separation of access to ones Higher Self. This helps to explain why during the taking of the Oath of Silence, which happens immediately after the candidates initial admittance, they are threatened with decapitation by the Hiereus when he lays the Geburic sword against the candidates Daath centre, located at the back of their neck. This suggests the severance of access to the spiritual realms of Kether, Chokmah and Binah.

Following the Oath, the candidate is placed in the North – the place of darkness and forgetfulness. The Hierophant speaks on behalf of the candidate and appeals to his undying soul to walk this path of putrefaction with the lamp of hidden knowledge to guide him. As mentioned earlier; psychologically, this state can manifest as depression (the dark night of the soul) and defensiveness, and it is not unusual for the candidate to experience these emotions at this point in the ritual. I have seen candidates who have chosen to undergo this experience, physically try to fight off the Keryx's challenges; such is their state of confusion and soul's isolation. Yet if you can feed the soul's seed, which lies waiting to unfurl in the darkness, by daring to look at the issues behind these emotional states, then the Albedo stage can commence. Thus the candidate is taken to the throne of the Heireus, where they are told that fear is failure, after which they are ushered onwards. It's far too late to go back, they have surrendered themselves to the Golden Dawn system and she is a harsh mistress and will poke you with the pointy sticks of your own creation.

ALBEDO

With the removal of the hoodwink, the candidate – the wanderer in the darkness of the Nigredo state – is called to the living beauty and gentle light of the Yesodic Lunar Goddess, whose lambent glow is caused by her reflection of the blinding Sun. They have symbolically been shown that they need to face their fears and to become aware of their own true nature, to take responsibility for the burgeoning and nurturing of the seed of their soul.

The hoodwink is removed and they are taken to the East of the altar, the location of Yesod and the three paths of Shin, Tau and Koph which together form the rainbow bridge, illuminated by the lunar light that hallmarks the Albedo stage.

The psychologist Carl Jung equated the Albedo (leukosis) stage with the contrasexual soul, which is given the name *Anima* for men and *Animus* for women. Jung considered it to be the phase where an insight into ones shadow-side could be achieved; the realisation that one is no longer at the complete mercy of one's own demons.

Images traditionally associated with this stage include Venus/Aphrodite, the white dove or swan, the White Queen and baptism by 'living water' that pours from the womb of creation. This holds the essence of the divinity that is in all of us, but that sometimes takes some literal soul-searching to find. The Albedo stage incorporates the alchemical stage of 'sublimato', referring to the separating out of the soul's essence from the murkier, muddied waters of human fallibility, psychological complexes and mundane existence. It is the recognition of a soul that has substance but is lacking in the lifeblood of the later alchemical stage of Rubedo.

CITRINITAS

Sometimes referred to as *xanthosis*, this stage refers to the transmutation of silver into gold, the "yellowing of the lunar conscientiousness." It is often represented by an eagle winging its way towards the Sun.

The candidate is now taken to stand between the pillars that symbolise Hod and Netzach. They are facing East, standing on the 27th path of The Tower – the tarot key that represents the falling away of earthly illusions. Thus they are now able to glimpse their own Tiphareth consciousness. It is the daybreak of one's soul seed which is now erupting through the earth and reaching for the light, heralding the Citrinitas stage. The Hierophant declares that the fourth and final consecration is to take place, after which the candidate is invested with the sash of the neophyte, which aptly symbolises the light dawning in the darkness.

At this point in the ceremony, the Hierophant astrally places the Godform of the candidate's Higher Self over the top of the new neophyte. Meanwhile the two pillars are psychically overlain with the images of the Goddesses Isis and Nephthys, who stretch forth their wings over the candidate – standing between the pillars with arms outstretched as they were over the body of

Osiris. This is the moment when the body of Osiris is brought to life again – in other words, the candidate is risen with their Higher Self connected to them and the final circumambulation commences, which reinforces the symbolism of the rising of the solar light in the candidate.

Jung equated this stage with the wise man or wise woman – someone who had accumulated knowledge and awareness of something greater. They are the realised Magician, a wizard of the Gandalf variety who often advises noble souls on quests for holy grails and magic wands.

RUBEDO

The final stage is referred to as Rubedo (iosis), the reddening relates to the blending of the soul with one's Higher Self or Tiphareth consciousness. Some may see this as akin to the idealised concept of Christ consciousness, or expect to see it in an Adept. This is misleading, for maintenance of Tiphareth consciousness whilst in the earthly body can lead to insanity. We reach for the red rose of Rubedo; we can even pluck it and share its scent with others, but whilst in Malkuth we still have to live in the body of an ass. Anyone who has experienced this can hold it no better than someone can hold water running through their hands. If anyone tells you otherwise, you should immediately run a mile. Following the Hierophant and Hiereus' exhortations to the neophyte about the symbols and officers of the temple, after their Sphere of Sensation has been ripped apart, purified, consecrated four times, and then reassembled, there is a final point in the ceremony which relates to the Rubedo stage. This is the alchemical change which involves the mixing of the Venus and Mars fluids.

Originally, the alchemical change involved a ten percent solution of iron perchloride and a one percent solution of potassium sulphocyanide. The former was known as the Venus fluid and sometimes the "Elixir of Gold". It was used as a blood-purifying tonic and a panacea against venereal diseases (diseases of Venus). A solution was also commercially used to etch copper, the metal of Venus.

Potassium sulphocyanide was used to detect iron, the metal of Mars, and may help to explain why it was referred to as the Mars fluid. Its addition to the iron perchloride creates a reddening, Rubedo. The redness caused by the interaction between these two chemicals was well known and was employed in photography to impart a red hue to prints. It was also used in nineteenth century theatrical magic where these two clear fluids were dramatically combined to make 'blood' when shock-value was required.

Whilst the mixing of these fluids occurs, the candidate is told by the Keryx that within the clear fluid there lie "elements bearing the semblance of blood, even as within the mind and the brain of the initiate lie concealed the Divine Secrets of the Hidden Knowledge." The Keryx then reminds the neophyte how easily this blood, this Hidden Knowledge, can be spilt, the body broken, with a guaranteed trip back to square one. This echoes and reinforces the Oath of Silence and warns the candidate that they contain the seed of their own destruction, and if they fail or abandon the process then access to the spiritual realms and their own Higher Self could be removed.

This stage is also practical. The candidate is given a visual symbol that from two clear fluids, 'blood' is created. It is subliminally suggesting that their own blood, or life force, can be transformed by the Great Work. This symbol is built into their Sphere of Sensation and assists in its own realisation over time. The mixing of the fire of Mars with the passion of Venus marks the creation of something new. It is the consummation, the conjunction of the Venusian White Queen with the fire of the Red King. It marks the transmutation of the soul's essence into something greater – the true realisation and actualisation of divinity within oneself. More than one European Magical Order used similar ideas based on polarity, to test the Stone at the Rubedo stage.

Jung equated this stage with the union of one's anima and animus and the creation of wholeness. It is fitting that the Keryx, the Mercurial mediator, is the one present whilst this operation is performed. Furthermore, the Keryx is representative of the hermaphrodite Hermes, composed of male and female, Mars and Venus.

ALCHEMY OF THE OFFICERS

This four-fold alchemical pattern can be extended to the three main officers and is seen in the colour of the tabards that they wear. The Hiereus, with his black tabard, represents the process of putrefaction. His station in the West is the "Place of the Guardian against the Multitudes that sleep through the Light and awaken at the Twilight." If you overlay the Tree of Life over the 0=0 temple layout, the Heireus is in Malkuth, the Earth from which all physical life is born and is ultimately returned.

The Hegemon, with her white tabard, is connected with the Albedo and Citrinitas stages. On the Tree of Life, her station between the pillars connects to lunar Yesod (Albedo). As stated in the neophyte temple opening ritual, she leads the candidate on "the Path that conducts from Darkness (Nigredo) to Light." When she gives the new neophyte their sash, which symbolises their awakening, she is embodying the Citrinitas stage with its first glimmer of light that heralds the impending Solar Dawn.

The Hierophant, with his red tabard, is the Rubedo phase. He is the "Guardian of the Dawning Sun" and as such embodies the alchemical process of fermentation, which gives new life to a substance, resurrects it. In the 0=0 opening, the Hierophant declares that his red robe represents the uncreated and created fire, the essence of Geburah (Mars) and Netzach (Venus) which meet in Tiphareth and create the Reddening. His station equates roughly to Tiphareth consciousness, Solar Light and the source of higher spiritual illumination.

Throughout the 0=0, the candidate has symbolically been shown the alchemical processes that must be mastered. The rough, unhewn stone must be refined and turned into the perfection of the quintessence of their own soul. Their journey through the Outer Order should help them discover their divine illustriousness, as their soul burns its way from seed to blooming rose on the cross of sacrifice.

Celtic Chakras

ELEN SENTIER

Here in Britain, we've largely forgotten our ancient, indigenous heritage to the extent that some people think there is no concept of 'chakras' in the Western tradition, but this is not the case. Chakras are found in the mystery traditions all over the world, indeed they must be as they are integral to life. They were well-known to our hunter-gatherer ancestors and the awenyddion (spirit-keepers) who led them in pre-historic times.

There is a strong body of knowing hidden deep in the stories and myths of Britain; it's the way of all esoteric and occult traditions that wisdom is very well hidden, often in plain sight. The awenyddion, the spirit-keepers of Britain, have held the tales from time out of mind. The wisdom follows the quicksilver pathways of the British goddesses … Elen of the Ways, the Deer Goddess; Arianrhod, Lady of the Moon and Stars; Ceridwen, Lady of the Cauldrons; and Brighid of the Three Faces.

They all have their parts to play. For instance, Arianrhod's name means "Silver Wheel", "Tower" or "Fortress". It comes from the Welsh *arian*, meaning "silver"; and *rhod*, which comes from the Indo-European root meaning "wheel". Her name is likely cognate with Proto-Celtic Arganto-rotā, meaning "silver wheel". It's possible her name may have also been Arianrath; in Irish, *ráth* means "earthen ring-fort" – taking us back to caers again. The Sanskrit word "chakra" also means "wheel", sometimes "fiery wheel". For those who can see, chakras often look like fiery wheels. Ceridwen is Lady of the Cauldron and initiatrix, as she shows in the story of Taliesin. Brighid has three faces of Smith, Healer and Poet that correspond to the three cauldrons, caers;

she is where the 3-ness comes together at the brow, the place of synthesis. I go into them in some depth in the book but, for this article, I'm concentrating on our most ancient lady, Elen of the Ways, for it was she who pointed me onto the track many years ago.

DEER GODDESS OF THE BOREAL FOREST

Elen of the Ways is the deer goddess of the peoples of the Boreal Forest. The Boreal Forest is, still, the largest forest biome in the world. It reaches from the tundra, at latitude 72, down to latitude 50, which is the tip of Cornwall. Once upon a time, all of Britain was forested as a part of the Boreal Forest which stretches all the way around the northern hemisphere. Canada, Scandinavia and Russia still have huge forested areas and these are the lands of the reindeer; in Canada they call them caribou but they are the same beast. All through these lands the peoples have walked with the reindeer, followed the deer-trods; the Caribou People and the Sámi still do to some extent; our own ancestors walked these paths too.

Elen of the Ways is how we know the antlered, deer goddess in Britain. Reindeer are the only female deer to carry antlers; they used to roam Britain when we were a forested land and are beginning to return in Scotland with the Cairngorm herd.

Finding Elen requires a lot of work, hunting and stalking, waiting and watching, listening. You won't find much about her in academic historical texts; to seek her out, you need to go to the stories and songs, the old tales, and ask her to lead you along her tracks, as the grandmother deer leads the herd to new pastures. It's good to go to places that have the prehistoric drawings from our ancestors to carry you on the journey-thread. Creswell Crags in the Peak District, on the border between Derbyshire and Nottinghamshire, is one such place; it has pictures of bison, birds and *deer* put there by our ancestors during the last Ice Age. In

2011, a drawing of a reindeer some 14,500 years old was found in a cave on the Gower peninsula but this cannot be visited at present. Other Elen archaeological finds are few and far between … two Iron Age antlered female figurines near Colchester; a tile was found at Richborough showing a horned female; in the British Museum there is a small, squatting antlered female figure holding a cornucopia and patera from the Iron Age that inspired Celtic artist Cheska Potter. There are place-names all over the country associated with Elen and they are well worth visiting to journey at.

Our ancestors followed the deer-trods and some of us come from family traditions that have held the old ways from generation to generation. I come from a family of awenyddion, spirit-keepers, and cunning folk. My mother's mother was a witch from the Isle of Man. My father's side were taleweavers and cunning folk; they also had strong relationships with theosophy, Annie Besant and Rudolf Steiner, so I grew up with that as well. Later, I went to the Alice Bailey work and found its teaching resonates deeply with the British stories from my childhood. The truths are the same all over the Earth; it's the telling that is different for each Spirit of Place.

CAULDRONS & CAERS

A big breakthrough came when I was studying transpersonal psychology. I was at Barbara Somers' marvellous workshop on the ten Taoist ox-herding pictures when she began to tell us of the three Taoist cauldrons that hold particular energy qualities … my mind began to buzz! In our British stories, there is the seventh century riddling poem, the *Cauldrons of Poesy*, which I was working on at that very time with Caitlin Matthews. It immediately struck me that the qualities of the Taoist cauldrons were so very similar to those of Poesy, although called by different names. Both sets of cauldrons reminded me of the three pairs of chakras, as known to the Indian tradition that I'd learned about in the Alice Bailey work. So began the path to the Celtic chakras book.

The old traditions of the East tell that the chakras come in pairs:

Crown – Base
Throat – Sacral
Heart – Solar Plexus

These three pairs all come together in the Brow, which is Brighid's domain, so I will leave that for now, you can find out more in the book.

The qualities of each of these pairs are similar to the qualities of the Taoist cauldrons *and* to those of the *Cauldrons of Poesy*.

Chakra pair	Chakra qualities			Taoist Cauldrons	Cauldrons of Poesy
Crown/Base	Life	Power	Good	Energy	Warmth
Heart/Solar Plexus	Love	Love	Beauty	Essence	Vocation
Throat/ Sacral	Light	Wisdom	Truth	Spirit	Wisdom

Here was 3-ness and cauldrons across the traditions.

A cauldron is a container, often a cooking pot, for both food and ideas; it is a strong place that holds energy together while it brews. A *caer* is also a container, a strong place that holds things together. The word *caer* relates to the Gaelic word *coire* which means "seething pool, kettle, boiler, vat and whirlpool" – we use the word "corrie" nowadays. Both words remind one of the idea of the spinning fiery wheel that is what the Sanskrit word "chakra" signifies. The Celtic languages share the Proto-Indo-European root; our language comes from the same source; Sanskrit is not foreign to the Celtic tongues but mother-sister to them.

I went back again to Elen; after all, she has always been my mentor…

Elen's best-known tale is *The Dream of Macsen Wledig*, which most people know from the Mabinogion tales. Macsen dreams of the most beautiful woman in the world and wants to find her. It takes him the magical seven years before he comes to her at her father's caer (stronghold) of Caer Seiont on the northwest coast of Wales. He woos and weds her. But Elen is an otherworldly woman; she is not human but goddess and sovereign in her own right. She *is* the Land, the goddess of the land, so Macsen performs the ancient ritual of all the old kings … he weds the land and promises to be its guardian and husbandman.

For her bride-gift, Elen asks Macsen to build her three caers – at Caernarfon, Caerleon and Carmarthen – and he does so,

I asked Elen to show me how her caers relate to the pairs of chakras … she gave me this table of correspondences; each of her caers stands for one of the three pairs of chakras, which each hold one of the three fundamental energy aspects.

Caer	Chakra pair	Chakra quality	Cauldron of Poesy	Brighid's face	Goddess face
Caernarfon	Crown/ Base	Life	Warmth	Blacksmith	Maiden
Caerleon	Heart/ Solar Plexus	Love	Vocation	Healer	Mother
Carmarthen	Throat/ Sacral	Light	Wisdom	Poet	Crone

LADY & LORD

At home, as a child, we always worked with the lady and the lord, seeing them as Elen and her antlered consort who hold the feminine/masculine, queen/king aspects of each energy.

Queen	King
Heart	Solar Plexus
Throat	Sacral
Crown	Base

Brow ...

where the queen and king are wed.

This picture is of a 2,500 year-old gold Celtic ornament, it was discovered in a woman's tomb at Bad Durkheim in Germany. If you look at the picture one way up then you see the face of a young woman; if you turn the picture the other way up, you see the face of an old man. It is the lady and the lord, goddess and god, holding the

pairs of opposites, the fundamental duality on which our Earth works, as our ancestors knew.

ELEN'S WAYS – THE SPIRAL PATH

When Macsen had given her the caers, Elen made pathways between them; in Wales they are still called Sarn Elens. The pathways between the caers carry the energy between the chakras and the pairs. In the Earth, pathways carry the energy through the planet herself as dragon, song and ley energy lines that connect the sacred places.

The Celtic path does not go straight; it is a labyrinth we call the Troy Town; you see it in the triskele too and find it in many others traditions. The labyrinth is not like a maze, it doesn't get you lost but *takes you there and back again*, like Bilbo ... but you never return to the same place, always it's a different turn of the spiral.

From childhood, I had been taught to journey through the energy centres of the body as part of the healing we did, and we always journeyed in a spiral. Many years later, I was delighted when Ian Gordon-Brown (who came through the Alice Bailey work) took us on the same spiral journey through the chakras in one of the transpersonal psychology workshops.

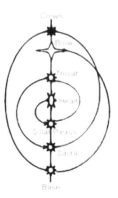

The spiral is important in other cultures too; for instance, for the Navajo it's the true spirit-path, both the straight line and the circle being considered human paths.

Coiling your way along the quicksilver path through the pairs of chakras you see this. You spiral through them from the centre to the brow, where they combine into the dual petals of energy the East calls yin/yang. Elen and her consort hold these polarities of energies for us, wedding the pairs of opposites.

As you wander through the mythologies of the world, you find similar concepts of the pathways that carry energy everywhere through the body. In the East, they are known as the meridians and nadis; Carlos Castaneda saw them as the web that makes our bodies and those of all living things, including the Earth; the Northern tradition calls this the wyrd; the Australian peoples see them as song-lines; Watkins saw them as ley lines; Hamish Miller saw them as dragon lines. Hamish and Paul Broadhurst also called them the Michael/Mary lines, recognising the innate duality of the queen/king that carries the feminine and masculine energy. They are the spiral threads that twine together like the double-helix of DNA.

The deer-trods are Elen's pathways, both on and within the earth. They connect her caers, the sacred sites of our land and the sacred fires within our bodies too. She is Elen of the Ways, the reindeer goddess of our land and we can follow her now as did our ancient British ancestors.

Circle Lines

MÉLUSINE DRACO

Many years ago, my friend and I passed those long, hot summer days of childhood roaming the surrounding fields and hedgerows. Then, we could disappear for hours, discovering the treasures of the season and enjoying the closeness of a silent companionship. Now some 60 years and hundreds of miles apart, we still share those memories of knowing where to find the first flowerings, and close encounters with birds and animals of the hedge bank. "Do you remember …" frequently crops up in letters and telephone conversations to recall to mind some indelible memory of a bank of spring celandines; the glimpse of a hunting stoat snaking through the undergrowth near the ruined barn; Easter violets; the chatter of nesting hedge sparrows, or more correctly 'dunnock', who often play foster parents to the cunning cuckoo.

Hedgerows were a prominent and distinctive feature of the landscape when I was a child, and the oldest were probably remnants of the continuous woodland that once covered most of the land. As villagers and landowners cleared the forest for agriculture, they would leave the last few feet of forest standing to mark the outer boundaries of their land. A traditional witchlet instinctively knows that these boundaries have a special magical significance, especially at dawn or dusk when we encountered a tawny owl hunting along the hedge in the twilight – or 'owl light', as we called it.

Some of our most ancient hedges are the remnants of such boundaries, perhaps even now still marking parish borders. Hedges were also formed to enclose patches of land to contain livestock. This would have been done close to a farm or village, and in many places these small irregular enclosures can still be recognised by witches of today, as indications of old field patterns and ancient hedgerows. The majority, however, were planted in the eighteenth and nineteenth centuries to enclose patches of land in order to establish ownership. Nevertheless, the older the hedge, the more we feel we are walking in our ancestors' footsteps as we search for magical and medicinal ingredients. Probably the leaves of the hawthorn are the first wild vegetable that country children learned to eat: widely known as 'bread and cheese', the young leaves have a pleasant nutty taste and we used to add them to our picnic sandwiches.

For both countrywomen and witches, the hedge was extremely important. A veritable treasure house: a source of food, drink, medicine, shelter, fuel and dyes, while numerous superstitions arose around many hedgerow plants. The special plant community that makes up a mature hedgerow also offers a wider range of food for animals and birds than most deciduous woodland, making the hedge a very attractive habitat during winter. After feasting on the autumn harvest of elder and blackberries, birds turn to rosehips and haws, then sloes and finally, to ivy berries – and this is where we become familiar with our totem animal or bird in its natural habitat. Here we often encountered a basking grass snake or, better still, a shed skin that could be made into a witch's garter.

The Romans introduced a large number of herbs to Britain, valuing them for their supposed supernatural powers, as well as culinary and medicinal uses ... and many of these plants now grow profusely in the wild. By the Middle Ages, the use of herbs for magical purposes was commonplace, and every village had its own witch or cunning-woman. A medieval witch was an expert in the identification of wild herbs, and from the countryside surrounding her home she would gather the appropriate plants for scenting linen, flavouring sauces ... or procuring an abortion.

Herbs were so important in daily life that when people moved around the country, they took with them the plants and the superstitions surrounding them.

Dr Harold Selcon reminds us in *The Physicians of Myddfai*, that by the end of the fourteenth century a different class of medical herbalist was developing – the apothecaries – who purchased herbs collected from the countryside by wandering professional herb collectors, known as the 'green men and women'. This occupation was a traditional one with a long history, and during the reign of Elizabeth I the Wild Herb Act was passed, giving the 'green-men' the right to gather herbs and roots on wild uncultivated land. Nevertheless, prior to, and during the First and Second World Wars, Britain grew large quantities of its own medicinal herbs; while a significant quantity of wild herbs were gathered for commercial use. The 'wild herb men' finally went out of business in the early 1960's; although, in December 1972, the *East Anglian Magazine* featured an article on one of the last men to gather wild plants for a living.

In fact, the use of common native plants in everyday home medicine is now almost obsolete, largely because it was mainly a DIY collection of first aid remedies, often passed on orally, rather than a written record. Although the growing pagan community has resulted in a resurgence of interest in these natural remedies, those who were fortunate in learning the language of the fields and hedgerows at an early age retain these early lessons in order to give a greater understanding of witchcraft in later life.

Mélusine Draco's Traditional Witchcraft series (including *Traditional Witchcraft for Fields & Hedgerows*) is published by Moon Books, an imprint of *www.johnhuntpublishing*, and can be ordered via Amazon. Her latest titles are also available from Moon Books.

Doreen Valiente and the Hermetic Order of the Golden Dawn

MELISSA SEIMS

Doreen Valiente is a name that I am sure every reader will have heard of. This inquisitive, intelligent, writer and witch was born in 1922, in Mitcham, Surrey, but lived for most of her life on the south coast of Britain. She had a keen interest in folklore, the occult and witchcraft and wrote several books on the latter subject. Always keen to expand her knowledge, she was involved with various different witchcraft groups throughout her life, and also worked solo magic too.

In 1952, *The Illustrated*[1] printed an article about witchcraft, based on an interview with Cecil Williamson, then-owner of the Witchcraft Museum on the Isle of Man. Upon reading it, Doreen wrote to Cecil who then referred her to Gerald Gardner, who was at that time the 'resident witch' of the museum. Her subsequent initiation and involvement in the re-working and writing of pieces for the 'Gardnerian' *Book of Shadows* is well-known and something she talks about in her book, *The Rebirth of Witchcraft*.

In the same book, we also find Doreen stating: "I had been a student of the Golden Dawn system of magic for years, long before I ever met Gerald Gardner."[2] Intrigued by this statement, I enlisted the help of Golden Dawn Magician and writer, Nick Farrell, and set out to try and find out more about Doreen

---

1 *The Illustrated*, 27th September, 1952. Viewable online at www.thewica. co.uk/Gerald%20Gardner.htm

2 *The Rebirth of Witchcraft* by Doreen Valiente (Phoenix Publishing, 1989), 200.

Valiente and her connection to that premier Magical Order, The Golden Dawn.

THE GOLDEN DAWN

The Golden Dawn has arguably been the most influential Magical Order ever to have existed. It was formed in 1887 by three Freemasons: Dr. William Wynn Westcott, Dr. William Robert Woodman, and Samuel Liddell MacGregor Mathers (who was the more magically-inclined of the three). Other well-known members included 'the Great Beast' Aleister Crowley, the mystical A.E. Waite, the creative W.B. Yeats, the magical Israel Regardie, and the gifted Dion Fortune.

The Golden Dawn's grade system is based on Qabalistic structure and consists of an Outer Order composed of five grades; it is this part of the Order that was originally referred to as the 'Hermetic Order of the Golden Dawn'. There is then an intermediary portal grade you have to pass through before moving on to the Second, or Inner Order, called the Ordo Roseae Rubeae et Aurae Crucis (R.R. et A.C.), which translates to 'Order of the Red Rose and Golden Cross'. It is in this Second Order where the real magical work of the Golden Dawn system starts. The First Order, Portal Grade and Second Order could loosely be likened to the three degrees found in witchcraft, with each being analogous to purification, consecration and amalgamation into the whole; although, the hermetic nature of the Golden Dawn tends to make it more cerebral than the Craft. There is a final, theoretical, Third Order that corresponds with the supernal triangle on the Tree of Life and it is said that no *living* person can enter this Order.

After making some enquiries, I have been unable to find anything to suggest that Doreen was a member of any Golden Dawn temple, or any of the related offshoot groups that existed in England in the 1940's and 1950's. However, in a letter Doreen wrote to Rev. T. Allen Greenfield[3] in 1986, she mentions that she owned some Golden Dawn notebooks that belonged to Frater Nisi Dominus Frustra. Evidence would seem to suggest that it was these original notebooks (along with Regardie's published Golden Dawn works) that she considered herself "a student of". But how did Doreen obtain them?

DOREEN'S ACQUISITION

It was the Craft historian, Philip Heselton, who drew my attention to a story in Gerald Gardner's biography, *Gerald Gardner Witch* (Octagon Press, 1960), attributed to Jack Bracelin but actually written by Sufi writer, Idries Shah. This book was written whilst Gardner was still alive and so, in a way, could be considered almost autobiographical.

Within its pages, we find a strange account[4] of how some Golden Dawn notebooks were acquired by a lady who was a witch. Reportedly, this witch was talking to her bank manager and he happened to mention that he was currently valuing for probate some magical belongings that were owned by a recently deceased doctor. The man's widow was frightened of the items and was thinking of burning them. From some snippets of information that the bank manager gives her, the witch manages to deduce where the doctor lives, and gets on a bus in order to investigate things further. After taking a pebble from the deceased doctor's garden, the witch uses it to 'create a link' and works some magic to ensure the safety of the notebooks. Her desire becomes manifest and the doctor's widow duly contacts the bank manager and, surprisingly, tells him that she knows he has a lady friend who is interested in the books and the other magical equipment, and that she can have them. The passage continues:

---

3   Letter from Doreen Valiente to Rev. T. Allen Greenfield dated 8th August, 1986. Viewable online at *www.geraldgardner.com/archive/valiente/index.php*
4   *Gerald Gardner: Witch* by Jack Bracelin (IHO, 1999), 162–164.

"There were twenty-eight magical books, two magical swords, two pentacles, and some other things. The manuscripts were those given to initiates into the Golden Dawn – a society started by the magicians MacGregor Mathers and WynnWestcott. They should have been learnt by heart and returned to the organisation.[5] One bore the name of Count MacGregor de Glenstrae, a name used by Mathers. She [the witch] kept the swords, but gave the MSS. to Gardner, who placed them in his museum."

I believe that the 'witch' is none other than Doreen Valiente and that this story, typical of Gardner's 'conceal-reveal' fashion, does actually bear some truth about how these Golden Dawn notebooks ended up firstly in Doreen's possession and secondly in Gardner's Museum of Witchcraft. Further evidence to support this can be found in the words that Doreen wrote in a letter to Gerald Yorke[6], a collector of magical items and Crowley's archivist. She writes:

"My friend Gerald Gardner tells me that you would like to hear from me, and has passed on to me a couple of letters he received from you, about some G.D. manuscripts in my possession … The story which Gerald tells – rather indiscreetly – of how the manuscripts were obtained is in the main true, though he does not know some of the details."

It seems to me, that the 'story' Doreen is referring to is quite probably the same one mentioned above and written about in *Gerald Gardner Witch*.

---

5   Gerald gets it wrong here. Each person was given a manuscript to copy, when this was done the copy was checked by a senior official in the Order and they were allowed to keep it. This was on the condition that the copy was returned to the Order on their death.

6   Undated letter from 'Ameth' (Doreen's magical name) to Gerald Yorke, which is in the Warburg Institute.

As suggested by the story, the notebooks were indeed loaned to Gardner by Doreen and placed in his Museum of Witchcraft on the Isle of Man, in the 'Golden Dawn Room'. As an interesting aside, this room was largely designed in 1951, by Steffi and Kenneth Grant with assistance from Gerald Yorke. This was about three years before Gardner had purchased the museum from Cecil Williamson.

In the museum's original pamphlet and guide we can find a small description of the books:

> *"Case No. 7 – A complete collection of the secret manuscripts of the Order of the Golden Dawn, a famous magical fraternity to which Aleister Crowley, W.B. Yeats, and many other well-known people at one time belonged. It was founded by the late Dr. Wynn Westcott and S.L. MacGregor Mathers, and claimed descent from the original Rosicrucians. Aleister Crowley quarrelled with the Order and broke away to found his own fraternity. The magical working of the Order of the Golden Dawn is founded upon the Hebrew Cabala, and its Cabalistic knowledge was kept very secret, though some of it has now found its way into print; but most of the contents of this case have never before been available to the public."*

Following Gerald's death, Doreen's notebooks seem to have been inadvertently bequeathed, along with the rest of the museum's contents, to Monique Marie Mauricette Wilson (nee Arnoux). Monique and her husband, Campbell, ran the museum for several years but fell on hard times and in 1973 decided to sell much of it to Ripley's in the USA. A lot of the collection was subsequently purchased in 1987, by Richard and Tamarra James of the Wiccan Church of Canada, and this is where Doreen's notebooks can be found today. There are not 28 books in the James' collection, as stated in Gardner's biography, although I suspect that the number '28' may be an example of Gardner's tendency to exaggerate matters; or perhaps the collection was divided up. However, as suggested by Gardner's story, one of them does bear the name *Comte MacGregor de Glenstrae* and Doreen did indeed own some Golden Dawn magical tools, now owned by her magical beneficiary, John Belham-Payne.

THE MAGICAL MSS OF THE HERMETIC ORDER OF THE ALPHA ET OMEGA

The notebooks consist of a series of small pocket-sized jotters with dates on them that range from 1902 to 1908. Several of them have 'official' printed stickers on the front and are labelled as belonging to the 'Hermetic Order of the A.O.' (Alpha et Omega). The earliest one, from 1902, is labelled slightly differently, with an earlier 'official' sticker that reads: 'Hermetic Order of the G.D.' with the 'G.D.' crossed out and 'A.O.' handwritten over the top. This would make sense as in 1900 the original Golden Dawn group started to splinter and the people loyal to Mathers carried on under the slightly revised name of the Hermetic Order of the Alpha et Omega.

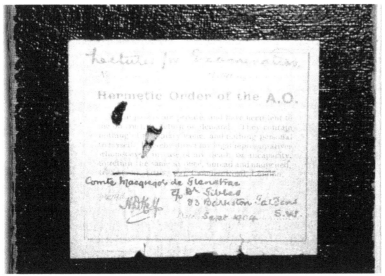

Cover of one of the books. Dated Sept, 1904.

The books contain the initiations for the five outer order grades: 0=0 (Neophyte), 1=10 (Zelator), 2=9 (Theoricus), 3=8 (Practicus), 4=7 (Philosophus), as well as the Portal and Second Order rituals. There are also several 'Flying Rolls', lecture notes, and examination answers.

Most of them appear to have belonged to Henry David Kelf, a pharmaceutical chemist dispenser, who at that time lived in Camberwell, London. His magical motto was 'Nisi Dominus Frustra', which is also the motto of the City of Edinburgh, and which means 'Except the Lord in Vain'. This is a heraldic contraction of a verse from the 127th Psalm: *"Except the Lord build the house, They labour in vain that build it. Except the Lord keep the city, The watchman waketh but in vain."* As a small aside to this, R.A. Gilbert in his book, *The Golden Dawn Companion*, mentions that there was a Lucy Margaret Bruce with the magical motto 'Nisi Dominus Frustra'. However, she was initiated in 1907, into the Stella Matutina, a Golden Dawn offshoot group created by Dr. Robert William Felkin and John William Brodie Innes, following one of the schisms that troubled the Order in the first few years of the twentieth century. As the name on the front of the notebooks is 'H.D. Kelf' and as these notebooks go back to a time before Lucy's initiation in 1907, I am working on the assumption that these two individuals just happened to have the same magical motto. This is not as unlikely as it may at first sound – in the early days of the Golden Dawn, people's magical mottos were often derived from their families heraldic motto, or those of a city with which they had strong ties.

Research reveals that Henry died in October 1951, in Poole, which is not far from Bournemouth where Valiente was living at the time. So, it seems likely that it was from Henry's widow, Clara Louisa, that Doreen acquired them. This was about a year prior to her meeting Gardner.

One small handwritten book in the collection belonged to Dr. Edmond Berridge, whose magical name was 'Resurgam'

(I shall rise again). Berridge was the Cancellarius (secretary and archivist) of the original Isis-Urania temple with Mathers being the Imperator (leader) and Wynn Westcott the Praemonstrator (teacher). Unfortunately, Westcott's interest in the Golden Dawn was causing problems between him and his employers and in 1897, he ended up leaving the Golden Dawn, although unofficially he remained behind the scenes as an advisor. Florence Farr, an actress and visionary, stepped up and took his place but in 1902, following further disagreements, she too resigned. Interestingly, the stickers on the front of many of these books could possibly reveal another of Dr. Westcott's successors; Westcott's old address of 396 Camden Road, London, has been crossed out and replaced with 'Dr. C. Gibbes, 83 Barkston Gardens, Earls Court, London'. Cuthbert C. Gibbes is listed in the 1901 census as having been a physician, and may have been a Mason. As it was usually the Praemonstrators name and address that was given on the front of books, it is possible (but not definite) that in 1902, it was Dr. Gibbes who held this position.

THE PATH OF LIGHT AND THE WICA

Many of the notebooks bear Doreen's handwriting. She appears to have gone through them and, in pencil, has added her own thoughts and notes on the material. What is clear is that the information in these notebooks influenced Doreen's thinking and the course that her own magical path took. In her personal diaries, and notebooks, she often wrote things in Hebrew, the basic magical alphabet of the Golden Dawn and which you are required to learn in the very first grade. Hebrew is not really associated with witchcraft, which tends to use Theban as its magical alphabet of choice. As Doreen had the notebooks prior to meeting Gerald Gardner, I feel sure that it was these that prompted and helped her to learn Hebrew.

Doreen also seems to have had a great respect for some of the ideas and essays that she read in these notebooks. So much so, she copied a large chunk of Flying Roll no. 5, 'Thoughts on Imagination' by Dr. Edmond Berridge, into her own, personal Book of Shadows, which she wrote shortly after being initiated by Gerald Gardner in 1953. Whilst Israel Regardie (some say with the help of Gerald Yorke) had published a lot of Golden Dawn material by 1940, this particular Flying Roll was not published until 1972, when it appeared in Francis King's book *Astral Projection, Ritual Magic and Alchemy*, so therefore Doreen's source was almost certainly the notebooks.

'Witch's Box Found on Beach' – Photo from the *Daily Telegraph*, 17th October, 1966.

Doreen's knowledge of the Golden Dawn also came to the rescue of some important Golden Dawn artefacts which had belonged to Maiya Tranchell Hayes, the mentor of Dion Fortune. In 1966, the *Daily Telegraph* ran a story entitled: 'Witch's Box Found on Beach'.[7] The box was found on the beach between Selsey Bill

7 *Daily Telegraph*, 17th October, 1966.

and Bracklesham Bay in Sussex, and contained quarter banners, sceptres, two embroidered stoles and Egyptian-style headdresses. Doreen's local paper, *The Evening Argus*, picked up the story and she immediately wrote to them to put them straight, saying: "These things are not part of a witch's regalia. They are actually part of the regalia of a very famous order called the Golden Dawn."[8] Doreen then contacted someone she knew in London (possibly Francis King) and facilitated the return of the items to the proper persons.

Gardner too, would undoubtedly have pored over these manuscripts and may perhaps have noticed the small notes that some of them contained with regards to whose notebook they had been copied from. In those days, there were obviously no photocopiers and each member had to carefully copy out the Golden Dawn's rituals and notes from someone else's book. Similarly, Crowley also observed this practice and insisted on people fastidiously copying out *The Book of the Law*. Such attention to detail had probably been spurred on by his earlier involvement with the Golden Dawn. This custom of carefully copying from others' books is of course also a traditional practice seen within witchcraft today.

From studying some of Gardner's own Books of Shadows, it is clear that MacGregor Mathers' translation of the highly influential book, *The Key of Solomon*, was one of several works that Gardner used to help him flesh out Craft rituals. Similarly, Mathers and Westcott are also thought to have fleshed out the early rituals of the Golden Dawn that reputedly came from the mysterious *Cipher Manuscripts*. In a way, it seems that Gardner was repeating a pattern; just as Gardner became highly influential and a crucial key in the revival of witchcraft, so too had Mathers been a vital cog in the revival of the Magical Order. Additionally, and on a lighter note, Gardner, like 'MacGregor' Mathers and Crowley before him, had also pretended to have Scottish ancestry!

---

8 *The Evening Argus*, 31st October, 1966.

One of Gardner's early Books of Shadows, often referred to as *'Text A'* and believed to date from the 1940's, is in the main a collection of extracts and ideas from books that had been published. It also contains a significant amount of material that was taken from the work of noted authors who were also members of, or very closely associated with, the Golden Dawn or one of its offshoot Orders. This included not only books that had been edited and translated by Mathers, but also the works of Dion Fortune, William Butler Yeats, Arthur Edward Waite, Fiona Macleod and, of course, Aleister Crowley. It is generally well-known that Aleister Crowley's writings have influenced Craft rituals, and for more information on this I refer the reader to the internet, where numerous sites[9] can be found investigating the parallels between Crowley and the 'Gardnerian' Book of Shadows.

'THE MAGICAL REVIVAL'

Recently, the media have been talking about TV presenter, Noel Edmonds, and his method of 'cosmic ordering', where he asks the Universe for what he desires. The power of desire is, of course, something that we as witches and Occultists have known about for a long time. The increase in popularity of the Qabalah (partially thanks to Madonna), as well as the 'New Age' movement, indicates that the time seems to be right for people to be more open to Magic in their lives. Now, more than ever, there are many different sorts of Magical Orders and witchcraft groups and traditions. It is my personal belief that the same 'energies' exist behind all of them and the differences come from personal interpretation and which magical framework you choose to hang your hat on.

---

9 http://www.cyprian.org/Articles/CrowleyBAM0.html and http://kheph777.tripod.com/art_wicca-thelema.html

The Occult scene has always been close-knit, especially down in the Home Counties, where like-minded individuals frequently bump into each other at the numerous groups, moots and conferences. In the pursuit of spiritual enlightenment of a more esoteric kind, we have always tended to influence each other, from MacGregor Mathers being influenced by Eliphas Levi and the unknown author(s) of *The Key of Solomon*, to Doreen Valiente and Gerald Gardner being influenced by Mathers and Crowley. There seems to be a sense of cyclicity about these things; of knowledge being passed down to be inherited and reinterpreted by younger generations. This is perhaps unsurprising, for Earth is not the only one to have her Great Wheel. We live in a cyclical Universe where vast galaxies, down to the tiniest sub-atomic particles, are continually dancing around in their own unique orbits; defined by maths, mechanics and probabilities, embedded in a fabric of space-time, all woven together, as if by magic!

I would like to thank Nick Farrell for his help, Philip Heselton who photographed Frater Nisi Dominus Frustra's Golden Dawn notebooks for me and Richard and Tamarra James of the Wiccan Church of Canada, who own them.

Frosty Forests &
Thought for the Future

*An Interview with Blue Fox of the
British Druid Order*

BLUE FOX

Despite the snow coming half way up my boots, the sun warms my face on this late January afternoon as I walk through the woods to meet Blue Fox of the British Druid Order (BDO) and find out what is currently going on in its eclectic and wonderful world … I have watched with interest as it has grown from being a 'cottage industry' ran near single-handedly by the enthusiasm and energy of one Philip Shallcrass (aka Greywolf) and any handy volunteers, to its latest incarnation as a real source of inspiration and enchantment to all those who come into contact with it. I once heard a definition of a friend given as: "somebody you can resume a conversation with days, months or even years after you saw them last." I believe I am fortunate to be able to call Blue Fox a friend …

"I am not a huge fan of Shakespeare," he says apropos to nothing, "but whilst studying him for 'O' levels, one line of thought regarding 'The Scottish Play' goes along the lines of he (Macbeth) would never have set out upon that particular course of action if the idea hadn't been suggested to him in the first place." I nod dumbly, not really following. "It seems to me that there has been a change since the winter solstice of 2012. People seemed so fixated on the whole 'end of the world' scenario and wondering what was to come next that, like in Macbeth, it almost became a self-fulfilling prophecy as a large section of the Pagan/Druid/Wiccan community were deferring action or taking little or no personal responsibility for their thoughts and actions as, at some level, they believed it was in some way out of their hands (the present & the future) and great cosmic events were somehow shaping them." And then the proverbial penny drops. I realise Mr. Fox is answering a question I put to him the other day when arranging this interview over the telephone, along the lines of "How do you think Druidry (and, by extension, Paganism – which for the sake of this interview I am choosing to use as an 'umbrella term' covering all branches of Pagan/alternative beliefs) has changed over the last few years?"

"I abhor the whole 'New Age' woolly thinking thing and kind of resent the insidious way it has come to almost infiltrate a lot of Pagan/Wiccan/Druidic thinking. At best, a lot of is misguided; and at worst, it is positively harmful and counter-productive to a lot of what we are trying to do and achieve." He assumes a mock Californian accent and goes on. "Like, Pringles are really bad for my Chi and my landlord was giving me a real hard time when I kept paying the rent late, and so I bought a black crystal and put it in my freezer box to 'chill' the problem." He (Blue Fox) now switches to a credible impersonation of Basil Fawlty at his most exasperated and cries out: "Lord suffering F*^k! Wouldn't it make more sense to cut down on the junk food, get organised and pay the landlord on time?!" A little calmer now, he resumes, "These people and that sort of (New Age) thinking seems to foster an almost endless capacity for self-delusion. All the great religions and spiritual teachings advocate cultivating a degree of self-awareness, be it through prayer, meditation or the practice of mindfulness, etc. But these people seem to have confused self-awareness with self-absorption and it's boring! Everything is about their 'journey', their 'healing' or their 'processes', and I am sick of it. They seem unable to differentiate or separate an idea from themselves. Should you challenge or dare to criticise their latest spiritual inanity or platitude, they take it as a personal attack upon themselves, and what with them being so sensitive at this stage of their journey … It stifles intellectual debate and, in my experience, does not move things forward, and I question its place in a lot of contemporary Pagan practice." For a second, I swear his eyes are blazing and then, as suddenly as it flares up, he announces: "End of rant," and a warm, disarming smile spreads across his face. I reckon it is time for my next question.

So where does the British Druid Order (BDO) figure in all this? All the time we have been talking he has been weaving hazel poles into the structure he is working on (wattling), building a wood store and future home to an earth oven as a compliment to the Roundhouse. He stops what he is doing, looks directly at me and in his best ironic 'ham acting' voice says, "Well, I'm glad you asked me that Steve" (remember, I'd 'tipped him off' previously as to the nature of the questions I'd be asking), "it's not all about me. It's not all about Philip (Greywolf, the 'Unchosen Chief' of the Order and 'Benevolent Dictator'). It's not all about Elaine (Wild Ways) or Adam (their I.T. 'wizard'). It's all about the members. About five years ago, a few BDO core members/inner circle sat down together and realised they had collectively something like 90 years practical experience as practicing Druids, shamans, Wiccans and 'whatnot'. We realised a lot of what we thought essential to the good practice of Druidry was either forgotten, not being addressed, or had not been 'discovered' yet. On a personal level, I strongly believed that the Pagan-Druidic landscape was a lot more interesting with Philip in it as, at the time, he was almost in a state of semi-retirement. So, Elaine and I gently coerced him into believing he was capable of making the BDO into something not only timely and relevant but necessary. He and I sat down and put our heads together and contrived a '10-point plan' of key elements we thought would or should complement what was already out there, and Philip promptly went away and did nothing. He carried on doing this for two years or so and then came back with a more or less complete system for doing Bardism or Bardic Druidry, running to over a quarter of a million words, set out in beautifully illustrated booklets. It blew me away, far exceeding my own ridiculously high standards and going above and beyond (below and around) what we had initially envisaged: I knew he was good, but man …"

He trails off and we both look up into the sky in response to the calls of three buzzards circling overhead, before he remarks, "I guess you could see those (nodding towards the buzzards) as a metaphor for us (Philip, Elaine and himself), the three of us circling together and weaving a sort of magic over these lands. While other Orders, networks and factions etc. were bickering and squabbling or becoming unnecessarily politicised or bureaucratic, we quietly got on and built the Roundhouse, put together a comprehensive and first rate course of Bardism and began to put together a calendar of apolitical events working with other 'shiny' and inspired people" (later elaboration tells me he is referring to the Blessing of the Tewkesbury Re-enactors weekend and The Mistletoe Foundation, amongst others). "I think what I am trying to say is, the Bardic course actively encourages those taking it to 'shine' for themselves: for them to find out what it is that 'turns them on', 'brings them alive', to find where their passions are and to actively pursue them. Obviously we cannot do it for them, but we can suggest and encourage ways of doing this so that everyone can tap into their own 'Awen' (source of inspiration). Often it's a case of a lack of confidence to try or crippling low self-esteem that holds people back. Through things we have personally found efficacious, drawing from those aforementioned years of practical experience, the BDO serves as a guide (I didn't catch what he says now as explosive laughter muffles something like 'or your eccentric uncle who … guffaw!') that can open your eyes and instil belief in you."

The infectious nature of the laughter and the spirit of openness and encouragement clearly inspire the Awen in me, and I phrase my next question in my best 'pseudo hippy' voice: "So where are you at now man?"

"Touché. Well, the Bardic course has been up and running for nearly two years now and is proving to be the screaming success we always hoped it would be. The first half of the Ovate Grade coursework has just been launched and some of our first Bardic 'graduates' are now taking this. This April sees 'The World Drum' return to these shores and being toured up and down these lands by the BDO and friends (see *www.theworlddrum.com* and *www. druidry.co.uk*), and the launch of an exciting new initiative in this country with 'Druid Hedge Schools' being premièred at Wild Ways in Shropshire (*www.druidhedgeschools.org.uk*). Philip also turns a venerable 60 this year and to celebrate this we are having one of, if not, 'thee' finest exponents of the Bardic arts in Robin Williamson playing at the event (again, see *www.druidry.co.uk* for more information). Obviously compiling, writing and editing the second part of the Ovate course will take up a lot of our time and, knowing Philip, he will then launch himself into more of the same with the Druid course."

"Ah, I see ... And the future?"

"Well ... See above for the completion of written coursework and you pretty much have it, but I personally would like to see a few more events, such as camps and retreats, where BDO 'bods' can get together, learn, laugh, share and 'groove' together. The taught component of the Bardic course alone is 'fizzing' with ideas, including a complete system of healing based on our research, and could provide a weekends workshop alone, let alone all the other manifold elements contained therein that could be explored. Both Elaine & I are very taken with the concept of the 're-enchantment of the land' and the stone circle we built just down the way (he points) is the first step in the physical embodiment of this beautiful concept and has already witnessed some moving ceremonies and ritual there: in order to build castles in the air, we need our feet firmly rooted in the ground."

That last sentence was delivered in a mock oriental 'guru-like' style (imagine 'Monkey' or 'Kung Fu' and you're getting close) and badly 'lip-synched'. I think I am finally getting the measure of this mercurial minded and self-deprecating individual, and 'Namaste' him for his 'wisdom/teaching'. A half smile and a cloud of cigarette smoke from the near perpetual roll-up never far from his lips, and he continues.

"Suzanne (Thomas), the 'powerhouse' behind The Mistletoe Foundation (*www.mistletoefoundation.co.uk*) and actively facilitating the Druid Hedge Schools (and recently responsible for putting a scarf around a hill in Shropshire – we all have to get our jollies some way I guess), has put together a copy of *Tooth & Claw* (the journal of the BDO) and there are even 'dark mutterings' of the re-release/re-launch of *The Druids Voice*, that erstwhile and well respected journal of contemporary Druidry. I have reason to believe another former stalwart of the BDO is organising another Druid Conference here in the West Midlands, the first since 2001, so there is a lot to be getting on with and to look forward to."

Aware that time is getting on, I ask: "Any further thoughts?"

"Yes. I feel I was a little hard on the New Agers earlier, but it does feel as if there has been a change in the 'psychic landscape' since 'the end of the world/Mayan Calendar' last Solstice. Maybe it is as simple as the fact it has finally stopped raining? But somehow it all feels a little 'fresher', that all that 'stuck energy' where people were waiting to see what would happen and whatever else they had invested in it is now 'free' – released, if you will – and now we can begin to move again: it's just a thought …"

He trails off once again, and I take the moment to take in the pre-Imbolc woods surrounding us. Yes, you can almost feel the potential in the earth. A few weeks from now and millions of tonnes of sap will rise up out of the earth and up into the treetops. The birdsong has already changed in its tone prior to the nesting and mating season and, by the time you read this, the forest floor will be carpeted with innumerable wild flowers and nearly every tree covered in fresh spring leaf as you prepare for your Beltane rites and rituals. Here and now though, in the pregnant stillness of pre-Imbolc potential and the promises of the year to come, I cannot but help but find myself in agreement with Blue Fox: something has changed. What we choose to do with this is entirely up to us, but it is near impossible not to thrill at all the raw potential, both around and in us.

Seemingly from out of nowhere, a wave of sadness washes over me. I'd hate to be standing here a year from now having gone nowhere and done nothing in the year to come. Those feelings of near euphoria and delight in the newness and potential inspired by chatting here are counter-balanced by a near dread of loss, inertia and inactivity. This feeling is fleeting, as whimsical as my host, and the shift in my reverie is now to a warm spring morning, 'dog's mercury' and celandine in counterpart to drifts of bluebells cover the forest floor around me, and every tree is pulsing with life.

Smoke rises through the thatch of the Roundhouse next to me and laughter and snatches of song compete with the birdsong. In my mind's eye, I see a harper just inside the door. What's that he is singing? "Come let us build, future ships in an ancient pattern, that journey far." The words of Robin Williamson's, *The Circle is Unbroken*, and it all makes sense. The timeless quality of the surrounds, a part of me rooted deep in the earth and an aspect of my soul going way back into antiquity. I am an ancestor. I am called to the here and now. I am a guest. I am as real as the spirits and will one day become one again. I am looking to the future: I am not scared by it. I am alive. I will not waste this gift.

As if reading my mind, a gentle voice next to me says, "It gets you like that. Fancy a coffee?"

Finished for now, we bid goodbye to the spirits of this enchanted place and make our way out of the woods to go and make friends with Mr. Kettle.

Gerald Gardner & the Ordo Templi Orientis

RODNEY ORPHEUS

Ordo Templi Orientis was first announced to the world in 1912, by Theodor Reuss and Aleister Crowley. Both men had been heavily involved in spiritual pursuits for many years previously: Reuss within the Theosophical Society and various esoteric Freemasonic groups; and Crowley within the Hermetic Order of the Golden Dawn, yoga, and Buddhism. Their vision was to form a new magical Order that would synthesise the Eastern mystical current of theosophy with the Western mystical current derived from Rosicrucian and other European sources, and thus O.T.O., or Order of the Temple of the East, was born.

The original rituals of the Order were derived from Freemasonry, but under Reuss' guidance, Crowley expanded and rewrote much of O.T.O. teachings; in particular writing the *Gnostic Mass*, which became the main public ritual of the Order, and which is still practiced all over the world on a weekly basis today. After Reuss' death, Crowley became the international head of O.T.O. – a position he held until his death in 1947.

Crowley had been quite the bon vivant during his lifetime. He travelled the world, dining with the cream (and sometimes the dregs) of literary society. He was frequently in demand as an after-dinner speaker, but by the mid-1940's he was becoming increasingly frail (he was in his seventies by then after all) and he wasn't getting about much. However, he still loved to entertain, and his diaries from this late period of his life are filled with notes on an almost daily basis about people who were coming to have tea with him. Notable figures who visited him included Captain Grady Louis McMurtry (October 18, 1918–July 12, 1985), a young American O.T.O. member based in England during World War II, who would later become head of O.T.O.; and Dion Fortune, already a well-known occult author, who was a real admirer of Crowley – she had given his *Magick in Theory & Practice* a glowing review, and acknowledged his influence in the introduction to her own work, *The Mystical Qabalah*.

A third notable visitor was Gerald Gardner, later to be celebrated as the founder of the modern witchcraft movement. Gardner had made the acquaintance of a friend of Crowley's, the well-known stage magician, Arnold Crowther (later to be husband of Patricia Crowther), who in turn brought Gardner to visit Crowley on Mayday in 1947. Crowley's diary records:

> *"Thurs I Miss Eva Collins. Dr G.B. Gardner Ph.D Singapore.*
> *Arnold Crowther rot G. a Magician to tea. Br. G. R. Arch."*

Extrapolating from Crowley's shorthand, we can ascertain that:

> *"Arnold Crowther brought Gardner, a Magician, to tea.*
> *Doctor Gardner is a Royal Arch Freemason."*

We have no record of what they spoke about, but it appears that they hit it off, since Gardner visited Crowley on several occasions over the next weeks:

> *"Wed 7 Dr Gardner about 12. Tell him phone Wel 6709.*
> *Wed 14 G.B.G.*
> *Tues 27 Gardner here."*

Wel 6709 was the phone number of another of Crowley's students – Order member and book collector, Gerald Yorke. Crowley wrote to Yorke on 9th May:

"This week I have had Dr. Gardner [...] here. I would be grateful if you would send to him one of the 4 copies of the Equinox of the Gods, which he has purchased."

The Equinox of the Gods was an edition of Crowley's *Book of the Law*, which O.T.O. had recently published. At some point, Gardner also purchased a copy of Crowley's *Blue Equinox*, which contained much O.T.O. material, as well as several other works of Crowley's, and he may well have bought these from Yorke in the same batch.

Crowley knew that he didn't have long to go in this world, and was desperate to ensure the survival of the O.T.O.'s teachings. It seems that he saw Gardner as a man who could keep the Order alive in Britain, and so he quickly arranged his initiation into O.T.O.

At that time, it was possible for Freemasons and Co-Masons to affiliate directly to O.T.O. at the same Degree they held in Masonry. Since Gardner had introduced himself to Crowley as a Royal Arch Mason on their first meeting, which was the equivalent to the IVO (Fourth Degree) of Ordo Templi Orientis, it was easy for Gardner to affiliate directly to that Degree in O.T.O., and it can be assumed that this took place sometime during their contact on May 11th.

Crowley also issued Gardner a charter to allow him to initiate further new members to the introductory Minerval Degree of Ordo Templi Orientis. The charter read:

Do what thou wilt shall be the law we Baphomet x^0 Ordo Templi Orientis Sovereign
Grand Master General of all English-Speaking Countries of the Earth do hereby Authorise our beloved son Scire, (Dr. G.B. Gardner,) Prince of Jerusalem, to constitute a camp of the Ordo Templi Orientis in the degree of Minerval Love is the law, Love under Will

Witness my hand and seal,
Baphomet x⁰

Baphomet was Crowley's magical name within O.T.O. The Tenth Degree or x^0 signifies his position as a Grand Master of the Order. Prince of Jerusalem, or Perfect Initiate, is a mystical title of members who have passed through the IVO initiations.

Another British occultist interested in O.T.O. during this period was W.B. Crow. He seems to have been running a small magical group and wrote to Crowley asking how they could be initiated into the Order. Crowley replied on 30th May, 1947:

> *"I suggest that you refer all your following in the London district to Dr. Gardner so that he may put them properly through the Minerval Degree, and some of them at least might help him establish the camps for the higher degrees up to Perfect Initiate or Prince of Jerusalem."*

(The Minerval Degree is the introductory or 00 of the Order.)

A couple of weeks later, on the 14th June, it seems that Crowley raised Gardner directly to the V110 (Seventh Degree) of O.T.O., issuing him a receipt for 10 guineas, which was the fee for that initiation. This is significant in light of Crowley's letter to W.B. Crow, since the O.T.O. system requires an initiator to be at least VIIO In order to initiate new members to the Degree of Prince of Jerusalem. The implication is that Crowley and Gardner had discussed their plans further and had agreed that Gardner should be elevated in order to ensure his ability to initiate up to that degree.

On 30th June, Crowley wrote to his second-in-command, the Order's Treasurer General, Karl Germer:

> *"England in particular is beginning to look up very brightly: we are getting a Camp of Minerval started during the summer if plans go as at present arranged."*

So there appears to be no doubt that Gardner was actively involved in O.T.O. at this point in time, and that Crowley held high hopes for the outcome. In the past, some have suggested that Crowley only initiated Gardner to get his money, but these letters to third parties show that Crowley was genuinely enthusiastic about having Gardner working within the Order.

Unfortunately, both Crowley and Gardner were to suffer severe health problems shortly after this flurry of activity, and it appears that the planned Camp of Minerval never materialised. A few months later, on 1st December, 1947, Crowley died. His papers were turned over to his literary executors in preparation for boxing up and shipping to O.T.O Headquarters in New York. However, Gardner wrote to Vernon Symonds on 24ᵗʰ December (note that I have preserved Gardner's original spelling):

> *"making me head of the O.T.O. in Europe. Now I want to get any papers about this, that Ahster had, he had some typescript Rituals. I know. I have them too, but I don't want his to fall in to other people's hands, I'll buy them off the Executors at a reasonable price, together with any other relics they may be willing to sell."*

Assuming this to be true (and given the other evidence, there's no reason to doubt it), we thus know that Gardner possessed copies of at least some of the O.T.O initiation ritual texts in 1947. Gardner also contacted Lady Frieda Harris, the artist who had painted the *Crowley Thoth Tarot Deck*, who was an IVO member of O.T.O.

Lady Harris on 2nd January, 1948, wrote to Karl Germer, who had become the overall head of the Order on Crowley's death, to inform him about the situation in the UK:

> *"G.B. Gardner, 282 Strathmoore Circle Memphis 12 Tenn. is head of the O.T.O. in Europe - Dr. W.B. Crow, 227 Glenfield*

Road Western Park Leicester has authority from A.C. to work the O.T.O. & the Gnostic Catholic Church.
Would you write to him.
Also Noel Fitzgerald 24 Belsize Road N. W6. seems to have been asked to initiate Mil Gardiner & may be a member."

From the date and tone of this letter, it appears that she may have been quoting information given to her directly by Gerald Gardner the previous month – I am assuming that Gardner had told her that he was lead of O.T.O. for Europe, and we know that Gardner had been in contact with W.B. Crow.

The mention of Noel Fitzgerald (who was a high-ranking IV0 member of the British O.T.O.) as possibly being Gardner's initiator is interesting. It was commonplace during this period for Crowley to initiate new members by putting them through all of the initiation rituals of the early O.T.O. Degrees in one day, or over the pace of a few weeks, and it is tempting to speculate that Noel Fitzgerald may have assisted Crowley in this. Internal evidence from rituals show similarities to particular points of O.T.O. initiation rites that would not be obvious through simply reading the text, but become quite obvious during performance of the rituals; so it is possible that Gardner was physically put through at least the Minerval initiation of O.T.O. and that these were not just 'paper degrees'.

Karl Germer appears to have accepted Gardner's claim to be running the Order in England, and the two men met in New York to discuss O.T.O. affairs on 19th March, 1948.

In December of 1950, Gardner wrote to John Symonds, Crowley's literary executor:

"I tried to start an order, but I got ill and had to leave the country. After his [Crowley's] death, word was sent to Germer that I was head of the Order in Europe, and Germer acknowledged me as such, but owing to ill health so far I haven't been able to get anything going. I've had some people

interested, but some with the army of occupation, and others lived far away, and so nothing happened. Actually, I haven't all the rituals. The K.T. ritual has been lost; Gerald Yorke thinks it may never have been written. I have up to Prince of Jerusalem. You don't know about the lost degrees, I suppose?"

(The K.T. ritual mentioned was the Knights Templar initiation, or VIO of O.T.O. It had been written, but Gardner had not been given a copy of it by Crowley.)

So, evidence shows that at least up until this date Gardner still considered himself an active member of O.T.O., that he was in possession of the texts of the preliminary initiation rituals of O.T.O. and had been planning on continuing to perform initiations. However, we know from his own "Book of Shadows" that he had already written the first drafts of his witchcraft initiations in 1949, a year earlier. Therefore, it seems that he was either planning on running both witchcraft and O.T.O. initiations, or that he wanted to get hold of the other O.T.O. ritual texts to use as source material for the writing he was doing for the witch cult. Perhaps if he had received copies of the other O.T.O. initiation rituals, witchcraft might have ended up with more than three Degrees!

What does seem clear from the despondent tone of the letter is that Gardner didn't realistically see much hope of his O.T.O. Camp succeeding. We have no record of any other O.T.O. correspondence from him after this date, and in March of 1951, Karl Germer asked a German member, Frederic Mellinger, to take over the leadership of the Order in Europe, and issued a charter to a young British member, Kenneth Grant, to form a new Camp in England to replace Gerald Gardner's.

Unfortunately, this new Camp was rather short-fived too, since it was closed and Grant expelled four years later; Noel Fitzgerald was put in charge of the British section of O.T.O. from 1955 onwards, a position he held until his death.

Gardner's 1950 letter to Symonds also stated about Crowley that:

> *"He was very interested in the witch cult and had some idea of combining it in with the Order, but nothing came of it, he was fascinated with some snaps of the Witches Cottage … I enclose a Copy of my book, High Magics Aid, A.C. read part of the M.S. & highly approved, he wanted me to put the Witch part in full."*

This is significant, in that Gardner himself states that Crowley consciously encouraged him to use witchcraft ideas alongside O.T.O. teachings, and that he pushed Gardner to emphasise witchcraft in his work. This is unsurprising, since Crowley had for many years been advocating the use of lunar, solar, and seasonal nature-based rituals. As far back as 1914, he had written to Frater Achad of the North American O.T.O. about a ritual of Isis that his Lodge had performed:

> *"I hope you will arrange to repeat this all the time, say every new moon or every full moon, so as to build up a regular force. You should also have a solar ritual to balance it, to be done at each time the Sun enters a new sign, with special festivity at the equinoxes and solstices.*
>
> *In this way you can establish a regular cult; and if you do them in a truly magical manner, you create a vortex of force which will suck in all the people you want. The time is just ripe for a natural religion. People like rites and ceremonies, and they are tired of hypothetical gods. Insist on the real benefits of the Sun, the Mother-force, the Father-force, and so on, and show that by celebrating these benefits worthily the worshippers unite themselves more fully with the current of life. Let the religion be Joy, but with a worthy and dignified sorrow in death itself, and treat death as an ordeal, an initiation … In short, be the founder of a new and greater Pagan cult."*

Here Crowley explains how he envisaged an O.T.O. body conducting its practical operations: Pagan rituals built around the natural cycle of the year. It's a position that is also made extremely clear within his text of the *Gnostic Mass* (written around the same period as the previous letter); for example, within the section of the Mass known as *The Collects*, which call upon The Sun, The Moon, The Earth, The Lord, The Lady, etc. So we can see that this vision of a natural religion had been part of Crowley's approach to Ordo Templi Orientis for over 30 years before he met Gerald Gardner – no wonder the two men hit it off so well right from their first meeting!

In their study of the early witchcraft movement, *Wicca: Magickal Beginnings*, David Rankine and Sorita D'Este show conclusively that much of Gardner's original *Book of Shadows* was derived from Crowleyan and O.T.O. sources, particularly the *Gnostic Mass*. For example, the ritual of *Drawing Down the Moon*, written in 1949, contains these lines spoken by the Magus:

> *"I Invoke and beseech Thee. O mighty Mother of all life and fertility. By seed and root, by stem and bud, by leaf and flower and fruit, by Life and Love, do I invoke Thee to descend into the body of thy servant and High Priestess."*

Compare this to the speech of the priest to the goddess in the O.T.O. *Gnostic Mass*, written by Crowley for Ordo Templi Orientis over three decades earlier:

> *"O circle of Stars whereof our Father is but the younger brother, marvel beyond imagination, soul of infinite space, before whom Time is Ashamed the mind bewildered, and the understanding dark, not unto Thee may we attain, unless Thine image be Love.*
> *Therefore, by seed and root and stem and bud and leaf and flower and fruit do we invoke Thee.*

Then the priest answered and said unto the Queen of Space, kissing her lovely brows, and the dew of her light bathing his whole body in a sweet-smelling perfume of sweat; O Nuit, continuous one of Heaven, let it be ever thus; that men speak not of thee as One but as None; and let them speak not of thee at all, since thou art continuous!"

Or the *Charge of the Goddess*, from Gardner in 1949:

"I love you: I yearn for you: pale or purple, veiled or voluptuous. I who am all pleasure, and purple and drunkenness of the innermost senses, desire you. Put on the wings, arouse the coiled splendour within you. Come unto me, for I am the flame that burns in the heart of every man, and the core of every Star. Let it be your inmost divine self who art lost in the constant rapture of infinite joy. Let the rituals be rightly performed with joy and beauty."

This is taken largely from the speech of the goddess in the O.T.O. *Gnostic Mass*:

"But to love me is better than all things; if under the night presently burnest mine incense before me, invoking me with a pure heart, and the serpent flame therein, thou shalt come a little to lie in my bosom. For one kiss wilt thou then be willing to give all; but whoso gives one particle of dust shall lose all in that hour. Ye shall gather goods and store of women and spices; ye shall wear rich jewels; ye shall exceed the nations of the earth in splendour and pride; but always in the love of me, and so shall ye come to my joy. I charge you earnestly to come before me in a single robe, and covered with a rich head-dress. I love you! I yearn to you! Pale or purple, veiled or voluptuous, I who am all pleasure and purple, and drunkenness of the innermost sense, desire you. Put on the wings, and arouse the coiled splendour within you: come unto me! To me! To me! Sing

the rapturous love-song unto me! Burn to me perfumes! Wear to me jewels! Drink to me, for I love you! I love you. I am the bluelidded daughter of sunset; I am the naked brilliance of the voluptuous night-sky. To me! To me!"

Gardner's February Eve Sabbat ritual from 1949 contains the section:

"Dread Lord of death and Resurrection, life and the giver of life, Lord within ourselves, whose name is Mystery of Mysteries, encourage our hearts. Let the light crystalize in our blood, fulfilling us of resurrection, for there is no part of us that is not of the gods."

Which is also obviously derived from a section of the O.T.O. *Gnostic Mass*:

"Thou that art One, our Lord in the Universe the Sun, our Lord in ourselves whose name is Mystery of Mystery, uttermost being whose radiance enlightening the worlds is also the breath that maketh every thingtremble before Thee – By the Sign of Light appear Thou the Sun.
Make open the path of creation and of intelligence between us and our minds. Enlighten our understanding.
Encourage our hearts. Let thy light crystallize itself in our blood, fulfilling us of Resurrection."

There are innumerable other excerpts from Crowley's works included within Gerald Gardner's other early rituals, particularly initiation rituals; so it appears clear that when Gardner was first formulating these rituals of his early witchcraft movement, the influence of Crowley and O.T.O. was a considerable one. O.T.O. scholar, Bill Heidrick, has alleged that as much as 80% of the text of Gardner's early witchcraft rituals may have been derived from Crowley's writings.

I think it is important that we do not see this use of Crowley's material as simply plagiarism on the part of Gerald Gardner. He was clearly considered to be an active and important member of O.T.O. at one point (albeit relatively briefly), and both Aleister Crowley and his successor, Karl Germer, granted him full authority to initiate new people into the Order and involve them in its teachings. However, after Crowley's death, Gardner seemingly felt that he was unable to fully utilise the O.T.O. structure, but did feel that the ritual teachings were important and could be inspirational to a whole new generation – hence his motivation to re-use them for his witch cult revival.

The growth of modern witchcraft has shown that Crowley's vision of the revival of natural religion was a correct one, and that Gardner shared that vision and applied it successfully. As such, I think that it behoves us to re-examine the relationship between Ordo Templi Orientis and witchcraft and treat it as one that can be both complementary and fruitful, as it has been right from the beginning.

REFERENCES

Apiryon, T. and Helena 2001) *Mystery or Mystery: A Primer of Thelemic Ecclesiastical Gnosticism*, 2nd ed.

Blecourt, W.D.; Fontaine, J.D.L. and Hutton, R. (2001) *Witchcraft and Magic in Europe, Volume 6 (History of Witchcraft and Magic in Europe)*. Athlone Press.

Crowley, A. 1947 Diaries & Letters.

Warburg Institute & O.T.O. Archives.

Crowley, A. (1919) *The Equinox III(1)*, Detroit MI: Universal Pub. Co.

Davis, M. *From Man to Witch: Gerald Gardner 1946–1949.* Available at: http://www.geraldgardner.com/Gardner46-49. PDF (Accessed May 19, 2009).

Fortune, D. (1935) *The Mystical Kabalah*. London: Williams and Norgate.

Heidrick, W. (1994) *alt.magick: Wicca and O.T.O.* Available at: http://www.luckymojo.com/esoteric/religion/neopaganism/9412.wiccoto.bh (Accessed May 20, 2009),

Orpheus, R. *Timeline of O.T.O. Succession After Crowley's Death*. Available at: *http://rodneyorpheus.com/* ae_id=110 (Accessed May 19, 2009).

Rankine, D. and d'Este, S. (2008) *Wicca Magickal Beginnings: A Study of the Possible Origins of The Rituals and Practices Found in this Modern Tradition of Pagan Witchcraft and Magick*, 2nd ed. Avalonia.

Starr, M.P. (2003) *The Unknown God: WT Smith and the Thelemites*, 1st ed. Teitan Press, Inc.

ABOUT THE AUTHOR

Rodney Orpheus is a well-known musician, writer, and lecturer. He is the author of the acclaimed *Abrahadahra: Understanding Aleister Crowley's Thelemic Magick,* and is putting the finishing touches to a new book on Thelema. He has been a member of O.T.O. for over two decades and currently serves as Deputy National Grand Master General of the U.K. Grand Lodge.

Giving Thanks

JULIAN VAYNE

A few weeks ago, I was sitting by the sea on the beautiful Devon coast. The day was bright, the sky magnificent blue. Meditating in that classic liminal space (where land and sky and sea meet), I took a breath of the Magical Aire. The traditional short-duration but richly decorated visions followed. Returning to awareness of my Self upon the shore, I was shown (as I was digging the spirit paradigm at that moment, though of course I might equally say 'made up in my head') a simple technique which I'd like to share.

Magical medicines are such that they are magical not only in themselves (as powerful molecules capable of radically changing consciousness) but also in that they are sacraments because they are deployed in a particular way and under particular circumstances. It's what we as magicians bring to the party, as much as the substances themselves, that matters.

One of the most powerful allies when working with these spirits is the sense of gratitude. We recognise that we are blessed to be able to have these potentially moving, healing, insightful, sometimes difficult and often exquisite experiences. What is important to understand here is that this orientation of gratitude to what is going on is quite genuine. And it's simultaneously true that this attitude is a tactic which we, take-no-prisoners chaos magicians, are quite happy to adopt because it gets us what we want (insight, healing, power, etc. etc.).

So, having come out of my trance, I wanted to recognise the sacredness of this experience. To write back into my unconscious my gratitude for the insights granted to me and to pave the way for future experiences of liberation.

ACKNOWLEDGING THE TRIPLE SANGHA

Hold the hands in prayer position on the crown of the head. Bring attention to the lineage of gurus who have allowed you to get to this moment in your own spiritual development. Depending on your style, you can imagine the sandals of your guru on your head, and their guru on top of them – a great line of teachers stretching into the sky. You might instead choose to imagine this as a community of stars above you. All those wise people, cunning folk, shamans, explorers and many others who, now, in the past and in the future, have been engaged with the philosophies and techniques of magick. There may be particular teachers, living or dead, which you want to bring your attention to in this moment. This act recognises that we are part of the sangha of these practitioners, in all their myriad forms and traditions.

Next, move the hands in prayer down so that the thumbs press on the Ajna chakra. With this movement, bring attention to yourself. You may think of this as the unique and indivisible diamond Atman of your existence. Or you may imagine the Self as being the confluence of many forces, acting in the past, present and future. You might wish to pay attention to yourself as a 'conspiracy of selves' or to recognise your own unique narrative (or a combination of all of these interpretations of the Self). In this moment, we pay homage to us – our individuality and sense of identity.

Finally, the hands are held in prayer at the heart. Bring attention to those beings that support you. Those who love and care for us, who feed and nurture us. This could include humans and other creatures we love, what we eat, the air we breathe and even people and situations we find difficult. However, the key focus here is on the sense of being loved and cared for. This is a moment for appreciating those aspects of the universe that provide us with this sense of being valued.

For some rites, this act of giving thanks does the same job as the traditional banishing ritual. The usual rules apply. Having spent as long as you need to with this practice, go and do something else. Let your awareness of acknowledging these blessings fade into the background reality of your daily life.

Historical and Spiritual Concepts of the Lakota Sioux

EAGLE MAN – ED McGAA

The Dakota wisely evacuated the Carolina Piedmont area after viewing the nearly total decimation of the disease-infested Atlantic coastal tribes doomed by Europe's early traders. "The White Man is powerful. You can trade with him and within a Moon you are dead … and … he is not there when you die."

1500–1600's, westward went the Dakota ('Allies', 'Friends'). They broke into two divisions: Lakota and Dakota (based on a linguistic difference). After two centuries, they were in the Dakota area, east of the Missouri and west of the Mississippi. The Lakota were always at the point of advancement, especially the two bands, Oglala and Sichangu, never far from each other. Five other bands formed the Teton Lakota: Minnecoujou (Minneconju), Hunkpapa and three other smaller bands. In 1775–76, the Oglala and Sichangu crossed the Missouri. They now had acquired French Guns – muzzle-loaders, cap and ball, single-shot muskets (learned from fighting the Chippewa and their Cree allies).

Prior to crossing, the more numerous Arikara lived in large stockade fortresses, mainly on the east side of the Missouri. Several thousand horses had the Arikara and carried saber-tipped spears, which a fairly large Spanish gold-seeking force had yielded, judging from the numerous sabers. The Oglala and Sichangu were in a quandary. The Yankton and Yanktonai

(Dakota) were pushing at their rear, and these Arikara were just too formidable to attempt a crossing over to the more numerous buffalo-rich west bank. Their answer approached from downstream – a steamboat! "The White Man can kill you without …" Grandparents remembered old stories. "No one will trade with the White Man." The warning was issued. "We will wait a moon for their horses and cross." The Arikara died by the thousands. "Anyone going into the Arikara camps to loot … will be shot or else we will all die too." Such was disciplined Lakota wisdom.

On the Plains westward, other tribes were no match for a musket-bearing, formidable cavalry. Two mounted hunters could now harvest enough meat that would take a village a week of organization and planning to equate. Earlier, the Cheyenne had wisely gifted some horses to a stranded Missouri ice-crossing Oglala and they remained allies all the way to the last major winning battle against the U.S. Cavalry.

For a century, the Sioux (as they were now termed), mainly the Lakota, would control the Great Plains from what would become the Dakotas west to the Big Horns and Rocky Mountain eastern foothills. Sioux meant 'Enemies' and indeed they absolutely were to anyone, including the U.S. Cavalry, for daring to cross them. Traders would supply them guns and later (pre-Civil War, 1861–1865) the lethal Winchester repeater (invented 1856), which could dispatch eight soldiers per warrior lost. They would ride equestrian or 'Mongolian' style, leaving both hands free for more accurate aiming, compared to the single-shot only handicapped cavalry riding with bit and reins. Try aiming a rifle while having to hold your reins trailing from each side of the horse's moving neck. See Schreyvogel drawings. The Army resorted to the pistol for close-in fighting, but it was less accurate than a rifle and had a much shorter range. Sioux would charge in after the second Army rifle volley from their single-shot Sharps rifles, which jammed often from a second-fired hastily loaded round due to a copper casing of the cartridge. The Army would hastily draw their pistols but, just out of pistol range, the Sioux would unleash their repeaters with deadly accuracy along with those who bore a .45–70. The results were disastrous for the U.S. Cavalry. Of, course white writers never portray what truthfully took place, because they refused to believe or learn from what the old time veterans could tell them. Typical military industrial complex collusion and corruption between the Springfield Arms Company to keep the advanced Winchester out of the U.S. Arsenal resulted in a longer Civil War, besides an added advantage for Chief Red Cloud's rifle-bearing warriors.

Gold was so plentiful that it could be picked out of Black Hills and Rocky Mountain streams and, along with fur, the repeaters could be purchased. Chief Crazy Horse's camp was attacked by General Crooks force of 1400 during winter conditions and dispatched by 250 Sioux warriors. Evidently, with the Winchester on one side only, this could never have happened.

The same-sized force under Crooks would attack again three months later in June of 1876, and suffer worse casualties by Crazy Horse's mounted forces of less than half; dispatching General Crooks to full retreat. Old time warriors state that Crazy Horse was chastised by Chief Sitting Bull for picking such a smaller force when many more warriors wanted to be picked. Crazy Horse held a Winchester and with a deadly smile, cocked the weapon and pretended to aim while bobbing a bit as if riding a horse, confidently stating, "I will stop him. You will see." He did so in a day and a half. About a week later, Colonel Custer met a worse fate, his command of 350 soldiers wiped out in less than an hour at the Little Big Horn River Sioux encampment for foolishly attacking a larger Sioux, Cheyenne and Arapahoe force. His dispatched command would lose half of 300 cavalrymen in about five minutes after they foolishly charged simultaneously from the camp's opposite end. A barrage of fire tumbled them from their horses into the river as they attempted to flee toward the protective cottonwood trees on the opposite side. Major Reno lived to adamantly complain about the Winchester's efficiency. Most of the captured weapons, ammunition and numerous cavalry horses were taken earlier by Chief Red Cloud's wars, 1855–1868.

Eventually, the Sioux were finally outnumbered and confined to the federally controlled Indian reservations. There, Christian missionaries would come in, boarding schools would be built to incarcerate and brainwash the youth to become lost into the white man's assimilation attempt and especially the missionary's focus to destroy and erase all traces of Sioux culture and their highly moral and ethical encouraging spirituality. Indians were unusually honest, simply because they believed their Benevolent Creator was All-Truth. Christians lobbied Congress to unconstitutionally ban our 'religion' – actually our spirituality. Spirituality is based on Nature which does not lie. Creator's designed math, physics and chemistry proves those facts. Creator's Nature does not 'fictitiously, mythically forgive' either. Last time I saw the devastation of a tornado after roaring through; it never returned and put everything back together again. Creator's 'chemical soup' make-up of the atmosphere or the oceans does bring serious, devastating change/alteration to these life-needed entities when an extreme amount of pollutant enters and remains within them. Planetary heating evolvement resulting and climate change is real. We are about to suffer the unalterable, Earth-destructive consequences of the powerful book Oglala conceived, *Black Elk Speaks*, which offered its dire spiritual-based environmental predictions, issued almost two centuries ago. The missionaries attempted to dilute and destroy that revelation because they could not control it, but failed.

We suffered severely under the over-zealous boarding school system. An extreme amount of time was spent on preaching Jesus to us, and working half the day in the fields, cattle, chicken and hog yards that made most boarding schools into gigantic productive farms. Very, very few, practically no academically deficient graduates went on to higher education, and were desperately unprepared if they attempted to do so. There were no Jesus requirements or questions on job applications, however.

World War I, WWII and the Korean War came and our young men readily volunteered. Probably, mainly to just get off the confining reservation was a factor for WWI soldiers when the Army came to recruit. My Uncle Albert was one who went overseas to fight in France.

The men from these wars came back and had a more confident attitude and questioned many facets of the restrictive reservation system. A smouldering ember, however, had always been glowing regarding our spirituality. The old full-bloods just could not and would not let go of the old beliefs in Creator, OUR own way and the old ceremonies that we utilized to honor Creator, Great Mystery, Great Spirit, Benevolent Creator, as we referred to IT and not a He or Him, or a She or Her. It was too difficult for those 'traditionalists' to believe that Creator (God) had an only child and now it was God watching over us and whom we were bound to pay allegiance to. Mainly, we were highly disappointed with the inhumane, anti-Mother Earth, heavily lying, untruthful conduct of the white man, even to his own kind. He had no concept of Creator as displaying so visually at least, how All Truthful it was. The white man simply disregarded truth. To a traditionalist, this kind of daily conduct would be an extreme barrier to a rewarding life into an awaiting Spirit World beyond. We also could not and would not conceive of this almost-as-powerful-as-Creator Devil, Satan, Lucifer force that roamed the planet so magically (not in accord with Creator's absolute laws of physics) and obviously had also a place in an All-Truthful Spirit World wherein All Knowledge resides.

Two brave medicine men, Chief Fools Crow and Chief Eagle Feather, attempted to bring the Sun Dance Appreciation Ceremony out into the open – out to the public. The war vets had started a new fire unknowingly. They questioned the white man, many moving off the Rez (Reservation). The military had given these men new trades and confidence. The missionaries paid little heed to these pitiful medicine men. What did they know? The bulk of the Indian sheep would rebuke and ignore their 'charade' – which they did. Silently, secretly, Peter Catches held a sparsely attended Sun Dance in the Bad Lands with a stunted tree almost invisible in a desolate ravine. The ceremony was 'legally' banned according to the ever-spying missionaries. You would lose your coveted rummage sale privileges, your kids bullied in the boarding schools if you ever challenged by attending 'the Devil ceremonies'. Finally, Bill Eagle Feather stated, "I am going to do the Sun Dance. Out in the open." Chief Fools Crow declared, "And I will do the piercing." The following summer, Eagle Feather danced beneath a cottonwood tree where a braided rope was attached. On the fourth day, the oversized burly medicine Sichangu would lay supine – face up, not moving a muscle. Fools Crow bent over him with a sharp awl. He pinched the chest skin, pulling it up to pierce and tunnel through it. Every Sun Dancer I have seen being pierced in such a manner never flinched (I have endured six).

Eagle Feather is giving his pain, "So that the people may live." A potential Sun Dancer may lose a daughter to a raging river. He vows, "If her body is found, I will do the Sun Dance as a Thanksgiving." A medicine person may hold a Spirit Calling ceremony to call in a Spirit (former ethical, moral, very truthfully conducted person during their time as a living two-legged human) while here. She is found snagged on a partially submerged tree. I took my vow, "If I can come back from Vietnam – alive!" After 110 combat missions enduring heavy ground fire at my F-4 and two separate surface-to-air missile attacks, one knocking out my port engine – I lived. I returned to thank the Ultimate Power.

From Eagle Feather's lone Sun Dance, which I viewed as a young teenager sitting beside my grandmother in awe at the ceremony, has now burst a burning flame. Over half of our Oglala Tribe has joyously returned to our Old Proven Way based on All Truthful Nature and we no longer have to live under the white man's deception with its constant lies, excuses and cover-ups. Hetchetuh aloh (it is so indeed).

Hyper-Real Spirituality: Pop Culture Magic

FRATER ISLA

Most folk'll tell you the use of pop culture iconography in ritual began in the 80's with Chaos Magick and the IOT. A few folk'll tell you it started earlier with people like William S. Burroughs, who was known to use a cardboard stand-up of Mick Jagger for "rites of performance". But I think it can be traced back to the beginning if you consider that at one time, even the Sumerian gods were pop sensations.

Those in the chaos current have always accepted the use of pop culture as being magically relevant. Just examine the successful integration of the Cthulhu Mythos by Anton LaVey, Phil Hine, and many others into the magical landscape over the last 50 years. Borrowing from any archetypal pool is considered okay, as long as it gets results. Devotion to an entity isn't necessary for it to be useful as a magical tool.

Recently, though, a trend has popped up that I've found myself right in the middle of: serious religious devotion given to fictional characters drawn from pop culture. I'm a member of the Sons of the Batman, a magical group that honours the Caped Crusader. Although it may appear to be a joke or an intellectual exercise, it's definitely not, and we take the worship of Batman very seriously.

And we are by no means the only ones.

Probably the most successful religious group inspired by a fictional source (outside of Scientology) would have to be the Church of Jediism. The Jedis have even gained tax-exemption in the US as a recognized non-profit religious organization. Their religion draws from the fictional universe of Star Wars, but they do not recognize its stories as any sort of scriptural reference. Instead, they see it as a point of philosophical inspiration, from which they've drawn the "16 teachings" and "21 Maxims". They definitely believe in the Force, though.

Jediism gained attention during the 2001 New Zealand census, after an e-mail campaign inspired more than 53,000 people to list "Jedi" as their religion. In the England and Wales census that year, over 390,000 claimed the same. The figure dropped to 176,000 last year, still outnumbering all the other "alternative" religions (including Atheism, numbering 29,000).

In 2004, Matrixism announced its arrival. It considered the Matrix films and related media to be "sacred texts", which are said to be inspired metaphors of an idea articulated by 'Abdu'l-Bahá', son of Bahá'u'lláh, founder of the Bahá'í faith. According to its website, there are over 2,000 adherents to the "Path of the One."

There's also a Church of Elvis, a Church of all Worlds (based on the fictional religion from Robert Heinlein's *Stranger in a Strange Land*), and even the first rumblings of a cult dedicated to My Little Pony. I'm sure with more digging, one could find many more examples.

Jediism and Matrixism were studied by Dr. Adam Possamai, along with other pop-inspired religions that he termed "hyper-real spiritualities". Possamai believes that these groups are the product of what he calls a "McDonaldised Occult culture", in which the beliefs that were once kept secret by groups like the Golden Dawn or the OTO are now easily found on the internet and bookshelves everywhere, making open comparison an easy task. Compound this with a desire to synthesize a consumerist culture with the search for a spiritual path, and you'll have some seekers finding a parallel between the religious teachings of more traditional sources and the themes found in fiction.

My own entrance to these ranks came about when I had the epiphany that my own beliefs were influenced not by Christ, Mohammed, Krishna, or Pan, but by the stories of the Batman. Without knowing it, by immersing myself within the Batman myth since the age of three, I was allowing it to mould my thinking as my ego and sense of morality formed. By acknowledging and actively reinforcing this belief structure, I began to experience a real clarity in my personal spiritual practices and the strange sense that I had possibly stumbled onto a kind of magical lynchpin. After years of experimenting with the deities of a variety of cultures, the myth that seemed to inspire me the most was the one I had so happily consumed since childhood, never imagining it to be divine in any way.

The switch from viewing these pop culture icons as mere tools to use in the practice of results magic to objects of spiritual devotion seems to coincide with a general trend. It appears that the prevailing themes of cynicism and irony which defined the attitude of occultism in the 90's have been replaced with a hunger for sincerity. Unlike their predecessors, the modern youth culture is unabashed by its reliance on consumerism and seems willing to integrate it into their spiritual life.

It's possible that rather than just being an interesting blip in religious evolution, devotion to the icons of pop culture may very well be the next serious movement in magic.

Irish Druidry and the Modern Druid Movement

LUKE EASTWOOD

Most Druids, and indeed Pagans generally, would be aware that Druids existed in Ireland. Fewer, I suspect, may know that Druidry/Druidism (*draíochta* in Irish means 'Druidry', synonymous with magic generally) continued uninterrupted during and after the Roman period that changed the face of western Europe.

The most common and well-known stream of modern Druidry is derived mostly from Welsh sources, rediscovered during the romantic revival. However, the Druidry of Ireland has also had a huge impact on the survival of Druidic knowledge and on the development of the modern movement itself.

The Romans swept through western Europe and in the process usurped the existing Celtic culture and their civilisation, beginning with Cisalpine Gaul and culminating with the colonisation of southern Britain. During this period, the Romans outlawed what we now refer to as Druidry/Druidism and imposed their own religious and social structures, leading to an acceptable middle-ground of Romano-Gaulish and Romano-British deities that we know of from archaeology and written records.

The indigenous Celtic culture was assimilated or eliminated in all of Europe except Ireland, Scotland, Wales and the most western and northern parts of what is now England. Although the Romans had long been aware of *Iuverna* or *Hibernia*, any plans to conquer Ireland were never enacted. Of all the countries in southern and central Europe, only Ireland remained completely untouched by Roman influence, few visited the country and solely for the purposes of trade or reconnaissance.

Likewise with Roman influence, Ireland was untouched by the Anglo-Saxons and, like Scotland, was late to succumb to the influence of Norman culture and feudalism. The result of this isolation was that the existing Celtic structures of governance, social, economic and religious life continued much as they had since ancient times. Changes obviously occurred with the passing of time and also as a result of a gradual shift from paganism to Christianity and the influence of Viking raiding and settlement in both Ireland and Scotland. However, the overriding cultural influence in both countries was that of the Gael, evidenced most clearly by the language (*Gaeilge* and *Gáidhlig* respectively), laws, dress and social structure.

Unfortunately, by the eighteenth century, when the Druid revivalist movement began the link between mainstream society and Bardic/Druidic culture had been severed, with only a very small number of Irish individuals or triads continuing their ancient traditions in secret. Sadly, the last of the secret Druids who had any recognisable claim to be hereditary seem to have died in the 1990's. Two Irish men I know of, via people who actually met or knew them personally, each claimed to be the last survivors a different triad – three members: *file* (Bard), *fáith* (Ovate), *druí* (Druid). Neither of these two men had an initiate or acolyte to pass on their knowledge to so, sadly, whatever secrets they had to tell died with them.

Despite this setback of lost continuity, Ireland was to have a direct influence on the re-emergence of Druidry in Britain. John Toland, credited with founding the Ancient Druid Order (ADO), was born in 1670 and raised in Donegal (northwest Ireland) in a Catholic family. After converting to Prostestantism at 16, he studied at Glasgow and Edinburgh universities, before moving to

Holland and later England. From the outset of his writing career, he caused controversy leading to attempts by the Irish parliament to have him executed for heresy.

As a political and religious maverick, he was considered the first of the freethinkers, writing extensively on religion, history, social and political issues of the day. He claimed himself to be a pantheist, which was quite outrageous at the time, although he wrote only one book on the subject of Druids and Celtic religion: *History of the Celtic Religion and Learning Containing an Account of the Druids* (1726). Toland was quite famous in his time but now is completely forgotten outside of academic and Druidic circles.

Despite its Irish founder, ADO (founded in England, 1717) was largely based on romantic ideas derived from Greco-Roman accounts, fantasy and the emerging Welsh remnants of Bardism, especially the dubious work of Iolo Morganwg (Edward Williams). Likewise, the Ancient Order of Druids (AOD, founded 1781) was romantic with a roughly Freemason structure. Other similar groups sprang up in Wales and France; and in the USA, The Ancient Order of Druids in America began in 1912.

It is was not until the mid-twentieth century that Irish Druidic remains were brought to light outside of the Celtic Twilight (in Ireland) or the academic circles of Ireland, England, France and Germany. The man responsible for this new awareness of Irish sources and the re-emergence of Gaelic culture into the modern Druid movement was a writer of German and Irish parentage – Robert Graves.

Ironically, Graves was a classicist and novelist, not a Gaelic scholar like his (Irish) father and grandfather (Bishop Charles Graves, member of the Royal Irish Academy and expert on Ogham and Brehon Law). In his 1948 book, *The White Goddess*, he made use of the largely unknown 'Song of Amergin' and the Irish Ogham alphabet, both of which date back to the pre-Christian period of Ireland.

Graves' scholarship and theories were in part based on false premises and poorly researched, second-hand information leading to intense criticism of the book, in particular due to his ignorance of his own paternal family's sound academic knowledge of Irish materials. Despite his fanciful shortcomings, it should be acknowledged that Robert Graves single-handedly reintroduced Irish Druidic sources to the mainstream of alternative spirituality and the Druid Movement that had largely forgotten their existence.

In 1964, Ross Nichols, the Chief Scribe of ADO, left to form the Order of Bards, Ovates and Druids (OBOD), having explored Celtic sources of and travelled around much of Britain and Ireland. ADO did not welcome his ideas of moving away from Masonic structures and towards re-exploring Neo-Druidry's Celtic roots, hence the formation of this new order, which is now one of the largest in the world.

It was Ross Nichols (along with Gerald Gardner) who introduced the eightfold festival celebrations often referred to as the 'Wheel of the Year'. Ross used Welsh names for the astronomical solar festivals of the solstices and equinoxes but he used the Irish names, derived from the ancient Irish Pagan festivals, for the four remaining festivals. Modern archaeological research and examination of ancient written sources and folk survivals clearly demonstrates that all eight festivals were celebrated in Ireland, if not elsewhere. The dates and practices of the modern festivals may not tally with those celebrated by the ancient Irish Druids; however, prior to Nichols' innovations, there was no official recognition of these seasonal events across the Druidic world.

Since that time, OBOD and other modern orders such as *Ár nDraíochta Féin* (ARD), BDO, Henge of Keltria, Druid Clan of Dana, and *Ord Na Druí* have all embraced Irish Celtic sources, the eight festivals and Irish language to varying degrees.

Thanks to many translations from *Gaeilge* of the eighteenth, nineteenth and early twentieth century's, the surviving mythology, Brehon law, poetry, place history (*Dindshenchas*), cosmology, Ogham alphabet, tree and plant lore, etc. has not only been preserved for the modern reader, but has provided a contemporaneous non-classical source for the modern Druid movement.

During the Elizabethan era, spoken and written *Gaeilge* (Irish language) was outlawed on pain of death. Many ancient Irish books were found and burned, but some made their way into English aristocratic collections or museums. Many books were hidden, by the Irish, under floors or in walls in order to escape destruction by the English colonists. Of course, many manuscripts were forever lost, forgotten or destroyed but fortunately many did survive in ecclesiastic institutions (in Ireland and Europe) and among the aristocracy until the prohibition was lifted.

Academics began translating from ancient and medieval Irish into modern English, French or German from the eighteenth century onwards – notable people we have to thank for this great legacy are Kuno Meyer, Whitely Stokes, R.A.S. MacAlister, P.W. Joyce, Eugene O'Curry and Augusta Gregory, to name but a few.

Without the pioneering work of these translators, the annals and works of the ancient and medieval Irish, that preserved much of what we now know about Druidic culture, would probably still be unknown and gathering dust in the world's museums and university vaults.

Indeed, a new wave of Pagan authors such as Caitlín & John Matthews, R.J. Stewart, Alexi Kondratiev, Koch & Carey, etc. have continued this exploration of the forgotten Irish, Scottish and Welsh translations, much to the enrichment of modern Druidry and our understanding of the Celts in general.

Sadly, what has been unearthed and translated is merely scratching the surface of what remains untranslated in university and museum archives. One can only wonder what gems lie waiting to be discovered …? Unfortunately, as Irish Celtic scholar Daragh Smyth explained to me, the process of translating these texts into modern languages is highly specialised, slow, labour-intensive and hence very expensive.

New translations and occasional new texts of Celtic source material do make it to publication from time to time (e.g. via C.E.L.T.) but there does not seem to be any organised programme or major investment in the process. Most ungratifying for myself and others, is the fact that exploration of the Celtic texts seems to be confined to the world of academia, with little or no access provided for the Druid or wider Pagan community. The academic world is generally not concerned with our religious or cultural practices, except from a historical or anthropological viewpoint, so perhaps it is no surprise that some modern Pagans' desire for new verifiable sources is not taken seriously.

I am hopeful that this attitude might change in the future, regarding Irish sources and indeed with regard to all ancient texts that remain untranslated. Given the re-emergence of Paganism and its new-found legal status I hope that increased respectability and acknowledgement will enable lobbying for the situation to change so that Pagan linguists, scholars and writers may gain first-hand access to the ancient sources that are currently unavailable.

In time, I see the modern Druid Movement being comprised of several distinct streams – Irish/Scottish-, Anglo/Welsh-, Breton/Gaulish-based reconstruction as well as the existing international and revivalist-based practices. The breadth of ancient Celtic thought and practice is only being fully revealed to modern Pagans now in this twenty-first century, long after the re-emergence of the Druids. It is an exciting prospect for the future, especially now that Paganism is no longer illegal or disreputable. As I do with Paganism generally, I look forward to seeing Druidry evolve and continue to rediscover its ancient origins.

Lessons of the Teacher Plants

ROSS HEAVEN

The shamanic use of plants is one of the world's oldest healing methods and, despite propaganda to the contrary, it is usually the safest and most effective form of medicine too.

In 2005, for example, the *British Medical Journal* warned that: "In England alone, reactions to drugs that led to hospitalisation followed by death are estimated at 5,700 a year and could actually be closer to 10,000." By comparison, in the four years between 2000 and August of 2004, there were just 451 reports of adverse reactions to herbal preparations, and only 152 were serious. No fatalities. That statistic equates to 38 problem cases a year resulting from plant medicines, compared to perhaps 10,000 deaths a year as a result of accepted mainstream medicine. Reviewing these figures, *The Independent* newspaper concluded that: "Herbs may not be completely safe, as critics like to point out – but they are a lot safer than drugs."

In America, orthodox medical treatment is itself now the leading cause of death, ahead of heart disease and cancer. According to Consumer Reports Online (www.consumerreports. org): "Infections, surgical mistakes and other medical harm contributes to the deaths of 180,000 hospital patients a year … Another 1.4 million are seriously hurt by their hospital care. And those figures apply only to Medicare patients. What happens to other people is less clear because most hospital errors go unreported and hospitals report on only a fraction of things that can go wrong."

Other studies reveal that adverse drug reactions are under-reported by up to 94 per cent, since the US government does not adequately track them. Death as a result of plant healings, meanwhile, remain next to zero. It is worth asking why these figures so often go unreported, who might benefit from this, and why the medical profession continues to treat people as it does, even with full awareness of drug risks and the comparative safety of plants?

More remarkable than their ability to safely heal the body, however, is the ability of some plants to expand the mind, raise consciousness, release stuck or damaging emotions and connect us more deeply to spirit. These are the teacher plants or, as they are also known, the entheogens: plants which are mind-altering, mind-liberating or 'mind-manifesting' and which reveal 'the God within us' (the more accurate translation of the word 'entheogen') – the extent of our power and potential.

Teacher plants are used by shamans worldwide in a sacred ritual context to divine the future, enter spirit realms, learn the deepest truths about themselves and the universe (although many shamans see little distinction between the two since, as they say, 'the world is as you dream it' – that is, each of us *is* the universe) and perform healings which go beyond the capabilities of Western medicine.

Working with teacher plants is like joining an academy of advanced learning and, like the professors in any academy, each plant has particular skills, talents and areas of expertise. Of the currently best-known teacher plants in the West, for example, Salvia divinorum shows us the true nature of the reality we take for granted, while ayahuasca teaches us about the creative possibilities of the universe, and San Pedro educates us in how to be human. But that is not all that these teachers do. They belong to the plant kingdom as well, just as every professor, no matter what his speciality, is also a human being and shares characteristics in common with everyone else through his humanity. Plants are the same, so everyone knows something about all others and can inform us about them as well as itself. Finally, all plants are aware (as some humans, and even some professors may be) that they are part of the 'mind of God'; an expression of the same energy that makes up the entire universe, so they can also open doorways for us into a wider understanding of life. There are four levels, then, of healing possibility with every plant:

THE PLANT AS A MEDICINE

Used in the same way that any herbalist might, Salvia, for example, can treat stomach problems, rheumatism and depression, among other conditions. Pharmaceutical drugs derived from the plant could also be used to combat diseases including Alzheimer's, AIDS, leukaemia and diabetes. There is also a magical illness that it can cure. *Panzón de Borrego* ('lamb belly') is a blockage in the stomach, seen as a stone put there by a rival, which may arise because of *mal d'ojo* – giving someone the 'evil eye' because you are jealous of them in some way. The person who receives such an attack is, of course, a victim of sorcery – but that does not mean that they are entirely innocent, since they might in fact have provoked their misfortune by bragging about their happiness or success and making others feel bad. Even though they are on the receiving end of negative energy, therefore, they may also be part of its cause. Orthodox medicine or herbalism might well be able to cure the *symptom* of the disease but by ignoring the magical component of the illness it would leave the *cause* untreated and so invite a recurrence. Used shamanically, however, Salvia can divine the cause of the problem and find an ongoing solution to it (for example, the suggestion that the patient acts in a more dignified manner in future so as not to provoke the ill-will of others) as well as an immediate cure. Even from a purely herbal perspective, then, the shamanic use of Salvia is more far-reaching and holistic than orthodox treatments and includes aspects of psychology, counselling and pastoral care.

THE PLANT AS A SPIRIT ALLY

Beyond their medicinal uses, plants can also teach us about ourselves, reality, existence, and the wider patterns of our lives. To some extent, this comes down to what shamans call intention or focus or 'having a good concentration' – entering into a committed partnership with the plant with the express intent that it will reveal information to us or pass on certain powers, and that, for our part, we will pay close attention to the signs that it sends us and the changes it makes to our bodies in order to receive its messages and gain mastery of the new abilities it gives us. The shamanic diet is likely to be part of this arrangement and involves certain actions and inactions, including restrictions on the behaviour of the dieter so he can learn from his ally and prepare for the expansion in consciousness that it will bring. Foods such as pork, fats, salt, sugar, spices, condiments and alcohol are prohibited, leaving the apprentice with a bland menu so he is not overwhelmed with flavour and can more finely sense the plant. It also weakens his attachments to routine, some of which revolve around meal times and foods. For the same reason, there is a prohibition on sexual activity, since sex is another worldly distraction and during orgasm we can also give away the power that has been building in us during the diet, which would be a pointless waste.

Breaking these taboos can lead the plant to turn against you so that it takes from you not only the power it has given you but any similar power you may already have had. In the case of San Pedro, for example, since one of the plant's intentions is to teach us about the nature of love, breaking the diet before it is complete can lead to the opposite effect – that is, to a broken heart and disconnection from life.

The typical shamanic diet lasts for fourteen days, with the plant drunk on the first three, while food restrictions continue for seven days in total. At the end of this week, a little lemon, salt, sugar and onion is eaten to formally break the diet and provide a safe boundary to the experience while offering protection to the plant so it can continue to grow inside you. There is then an after-diet for a further week and although the same restrictions apply to sex, alcohol, pork and strong spices, other foods can be eaten.

The biggest challenge for a Westerner undertaking this diet is often not the prohibitions themselves but accepting that plant consciousness can be experienced at all. We are born into the social paradigm that surrounds us with its beliefs and myths and the institutions which support its view of the world, and it is not within ours to easily accept that other beings (plants, spirits, animals) have souls or are capable of teaching us anything we don't already know. As we embark on the diet then, we often need to question some of our most deeply ingrained assumptions and allow that other forms of reality are possible.

For shamans, this is not such a problem since, for them, the world we perceive through our senses is just one description of a vast and mysterious unseen and not an absolute fact. Michael Harner writes, for example, that for the Jivaro Tribe of the Ecuadorian rainforests, "the normal waking life is explicitly viewed as 'false' or 'a lie' and it is firmly believed that truth about causality is to be found by entering the supernatural world, or what the Jivaro view as the 'real world', for they feel that the events which take place within it, underlie and are the basis for many of the surface manifestations and mysteries of daily life." Mazatec shaman, Maria Sabina, said much the same: "There is a world beyond ours, a world that is far away, nearby and invisible, and there is where God lives, where the dead live and the spirits and the saints. A world where everything has already happened, and everything is known. That world talks. It has a language of its own." The language of this world is what we learn through the diet.

AS A GUIDE TO THE SPIRITS OF OTHER PLANTS

Once it is a part of him, the plant ally begins to teach the shaman about itself, about other plants and about how to heal (the Mazatecs believe, for example, that Salvia will carry the apprentice to the 'tree of knowledge' in Heaven, where all healing plants grow and where saints and angels will instruct him in their uses).

All plants are part of the same kingdom, that is, they have an affinity with all others and know something about the specific powers of each. The plant as an ally, then, is more than just a healer in its own right, it becomes for the shaman a guide to the spirit world in general and an ambassador which will act on his behalf and introduce him to other plants. In my book, *Drinking the Four Winds*, for example, I talk about a long shamanic diet I did with the San Pedro cactus and how, during an ayahuasca ceremony to meet its spirit, it introduced me to a number of others that it wanted me to diet, including tobacco, rose, the Amazonian plants jergon sacha and chanca piedra, lime and Salvia. In this way, the shaman becomes knowledgeable about a range of plants and their healing uses and has a guide that he can call upon to lead him to those that he needs to heal any patient, even if he is unfamiliar with the patient's illness or the plants he may need to help him.

THE PLANT AS GATEWAY TO THE VOID, WHERE WE LEARN THE DEEPEST SECRETS OF ALL

Teacher plants, used ceremonially, lead the adept away from social conventions and consensus reality and teach him the secrets and mysteries which underpin our lives. Perhaps the greatest of these is that there is nothing to the universe except what we make of it. In this sense, we are God. But there is also something else: some other force or entity which is beyond us and which, perhaps, will always remain unknown.

THE QUICKENING: A TIMELINE OF WESTERN CONSCIOUSNESS

In shamanic terms (and as explorers of consciousness discover for themselves), all teacher plants, then, have a personality and purpose. Ayahuasca takes us out of the limited, Earthbound view we have of ourselves and into the wider spiritual universe, for example, so we can explore the fullness of our potential; while San Pedro brings us back to Earth with a new spiritual consciousness and reconnects us with our home so we see our world and ourselves as ensouled.

Where these realisations take us as the plants begin their pilgrimage from a shamanic context and into Western awareness – that is, how their intelligence begins to subtly inform our scientific and rational endeavours – is interesting too. Ayahuasca has a long history of use by the shamans of the Amazon, for example, but only really began its migration to the Western mind in the 1950's and 60's. Once there, it started to teach us, based on its purpose, about what was important as our next evolutionary step. Run through our rational-scientific filters, that could mean only one thing: ayahuasca took us to the moon and began our slow drift into space. San Pedro has similarly been used by the shamans of the Andres for thousands of years but it only began to come to Western attention in the 1980's. The outcome of its Earth-based perspective, washed through our 'thinking brains' once again, was the birth of the environmental movement and the emergence of green politics. In this way, teacher plants have always been leading us and there are practical outcomes as their spirits fuse subtly with ours.

What, then, are we to make of Salvia, probably the most important and challenging plant of our age? What is its purpose? What does it teach and where is it leading us? The plant first came to our attention in the 1990's, through the work of Daniel Siebert, who was the first person to extract salvinorin (its 'active ingredient') from it; but in terms of Western awareness, it may even be the best-known of the three. It took ayahuasca 60 years to achieve Western awareness; 30 years (half the time as ayahuasca) for San Pedro to achieve notoriety; and around 15 years for Salvia to establish itself. 60 years … 30 years … 15 years. Does anyone else see a pattern here? A quickening? Almost as if things are speeding up towards an endgame.

And perhaps they are because Salvia's teachings take us away from the Earth, and even the known universe, into a quantum realm of time travel and other dimensions. Ayahuasca gave us the cosmos within ourselves, San Pedro gave us the spirit of the Earth, but Salvia gives us the void and the question 'who are we really?' It also suggests that we may not have long to answer it so we should start to get 'real' now.

Marions Musings

MARION PEARCE

INTRODUCING THE WORLD OF THE PIXIE

Spring is here, the summer and winter gone, a fleeting memory. The days are lengthening, frosts line the air. The leaves are budding. There is still cold though, and the warm flames of a crackling open fire are beckoning. The nights are drawing in. Thoughts turn to storytelling around a cracking campfire.

A favourite for storytelling is that of the beings of the otherworld. One of the popular folklore creatures is that of the pixie. This mischievous sprite is part of a whole group of impish beings, some of which are: the north county brownie, the Devon pixy, the fairy, elf, goblin, Puck, Robin Goodfellow, the Irish leprechaun, the German kobold, and the Scandinavian troll. In Cornwall they are known as pisgies, in Somerset they are pixies, and in Dorset they are called pexies. There are many ancient names for this impish fellow.

I shall look in further detail at the Devon Pixy found on the wild Dartmoor moors. The Victorian writer, William Crossing's book, *Tales of the Dartmoor Pixies*, written in 1890, does go into great detail about these fascinating creatures. On the first page he remarks:

> "Among the superstitions of bygone times which still linger in Devonshire, the ideas regarding the pixies are undoubtedly the most interesting and romantic. Although the faith of the peasantry in the ability of these 'little people' to exercise control over their domestic arrangements is less firm than yore, yet a notion still prevails that ill-luck will certainly overtake the

> *hapless wight who is so unfortunate as to offend any of these diminutive elves."*

There is an old verse from Dartmoor describing these sprites:

> *'Thar be piskies up to Dartymoor*
> *And 'tidn't no good you say thar baint*
> *I've felt um grauping at my heart*
> *I've heard their voices calling faint.'*

In Devon, countless tourist shops sell model pixies, but what is behind this impish creature? For pure mischief, the Devonshire pixy lures people into bogs specially bedecked for the purpose with a waving sea of 'pixy grass' – the old Dartmoor name for the bog cotton plant, eriophorum. Old tales abound of people having been pixy lead to being lost and abandoned in the wild, featureless wastes of the Dartmoor plains. In this area of the country, the phrase, "I was properly pixy-led," is still used by someone who has inexplicably lost their way. The way to stop this happening was to turn ones cloak inside out. This was, of course, in the days when you wore cloaks. I do not know if the same protection would be offered to somebody who turned their modern coats inside out.

Legends of pixies abound on the moors. One of these tales centers on the Dartmoor spring, Fitz's Well. Here, a young couple returning home from chapel at Halstock, travelled late through the windswept moor. They encountered the pixies who evoked the dense mist, bringing it down on the pair so they could not find their way. Round and round in circles they rode, they were well and truly pixy led. On reaching the welcoming, fresh waters of the well, they dismounted, turned their cloaks, watered their horses and drank the ice cold draught of water from the well. This has miraculous results. Immediately, the mist lifted and they could see Okehampton lying below and were able to make their way safely off the moor. The man was so grateful for having escaped such an ordeal that he erected a granite stone cross, bearing a small incised cross between the arms, by the spring as a testament to their delivery.

The well soon became known as a magical well and on Easter morning, any youngster visiting the well could learn their destiny. Young women were known to trudge down the long steep hill from Okehampton to learn who they will marry in the depths of the well at Easter morning.

To confuse matters, there is another Fitz's Well but, over the years, the name has changed to Fice's Well. This well too is connected to the pixies. It is sited just outside of the Dartmoor town of Princetown, near the prison. This legend dates back to 1568. John Fitz and his wife were riding on the moor, they were enveloped by a thick swirling mist, totally lost and pixy led. But chancing to light upon a spring, they had no sooner tasted of the magical, refreshing water, than all difficulty about the matter vanished, and they were able to proceed without difficulty. Out of gratitude, they commemorated their delivery by protecting the potent waters from defilement by erecting a small stone canopied enclosure over Fice's Well, upon which are carved the initials 'I.F.' and the date 1568. Today, the well is to be found on reclaimed land, once used by the Dartmoor Prison Authorities.

Many local Dartmoor spots are named after the pixies. One of these is called Pixies Cave, near the town of Sheepstor. It is beautifully described by William Cossing in all its ethereal qualities:

> "Not far from the point of confluence of the two branches of the Mew rises 'Sheepstor's dark-browed rock,' and on the slope of the tor, on the side on which the village lies, is a vast clatter of boulders. Amid this is a narrow opening between two upright rocks, which will admit the visitor, though not without a little difficulty, into a small grotto, celebrated in local legend, and known as the Pixies' Cave. On entering the cleft, we shall

find that the passage, which is only a few feet in length, turns abruptly to the left, and we shall also have to descend a little, as the floor of the cave is several feet lower than the rock at the entrance. This turning leads immediately into the cave, which we shall find to be a small square apartment capable of containing several persons, but scarcely high enough to permit us to stand upright. On our left as we enter is a rude stone seat, and in the furthest corner a low narrow passage, extending for some little distance, is discoverable."

It is said that this magical cave was the hiding place of fugitive royalists during the Civil War, although it is best-known as the haunt of the mysterious pixies. It is customary to leave an offering to the pixies before you leave their mysterious cave. This is important. They like pins. Failing that, a small piece of material for the little peoples clothing, or some ribbon.

There are other places in the bleak windswept moors named after these mischievous imps. Pixies Parlour is a pile of old tumbled boulders beside the public footpath leading from the town of Sandypark to the Fingle Gorge and Bridge. Upon one of these great rocks rests a tired, gnarled and deformed old Scots pine, its trunk contorted into a comfortable sitting posture, as though weariness had overcome the tree while waiting for the 'little people' who used to frolic around its feet.

Yet another old romantic place in Dartmoor associated with the pixies is the Puggie Stone. This enormous single boulder lies beside Holy Street, that long Chagford Lane which leads moorwards. The name Puggie is associated with Puck, mentioned by William Shakespeare, and a famous pixie. Through the names Puck, Pucksie, and Puggie we eventually arrive at pixie. Indeed, the word pixy is derived from puck or pwc, meaning sprite or goblin. It is interesting to speculate that Shakespeare was familiar with pixie lore.

Shakespeare describes Puck:

"Are you not he,
That frights the maidens of the villagery;
Skim milk; and sometimes labour in the quern;
And bootless make the breathless housewife churn;
And sometime make the drink to bear no barm;
Mislead night-wanderers, laughing at their harm?
Those that Hobgoblin call you, and sweet Puck,
You do their work, and they shall have good luck:
Are not you he?"

To which Puck replies:

"Thou speak'st aright;
I am that merry wanderer of the night."

But the moorland pixies could help as well as hinder. To go back to the great Devonshire local historian and folklorist, William Cossing:

"But if the elfin sprites occasionally mislead the traveller, they more than make up for it, if it be true as we are sometimes told, that they indicate spots where metals may be found. Beneath the fairy rings where they dance and sing by night, the miner has only to dig and he will be sure to hit upon a precious lode; that the goblins themselves occasionally engage in such a pursuit almost seems to be the case, for it is told how they may be heard knocking within the rocks. And if you apply your ear to the granite sides of some of the tors of the moor, it is said you may hear the pixies ringing their bells within; the 'pixies' in this case probably being the faint echo of some distant village peal."

The Devon pixies are mysterious little folk, they have permeated folklore and could be still living in the ancient countryside near you.

Merl and Dion

JOHN DAVIES

Most accounts of the marriage of Dion Fortune and Thomas Penry Evans emphasise that they were both extremely strong-willed characters, who struck sparks off each other. Although the accepted view seems to be that they were quite fond of each other, their marriage was notorious for furious quarrels.

Thomas Penry Evans was extremely ambitious. He was a very powerfully motivated social climber. This has nothing to do with "Keltic Twylight". It is about very hard reality. His father was a "tin shearer" in Llanelli. I'd better expand on that. The old Welsh working class is not altogether easy to understand if you never knew it at first hand.

In *Priestess*, his biography of Dion Fortune, Alan Richardson refers to the "miners of Llanelli". But by the 1930s, mining was not Llanelli's principal industry. Instead, the town made high-quality specialised steel, specifically tinplate, for which it was famous. However, decades earlier, Llanelli had indeed been a mining town, and as a result, it sits above a warren of flooded tunnels. Coal-mining was the main industry in the Gwendraeth Valley, a few miles up-country from Llanelli. My father's family came from there. Richardson also refers to the "Tin-Miners of Wales". There never were any. Tin is mined in Cornwall. Wales mined coal. So what was this culture like? To give you a flavour of the old valley's coal-mining culture, in the closing phases of the Scargill coal strike (1984–85), when most of Nottinghamshire and about half of his own region of Yorkshire had drifted back to work, there were just four miners at work in the entire South Wales coalfield. They were at the Cynheidre pit near Pontyberem.

The villagers were terribly embarrassed to be harbouring these four traitors. They were at pains to explain they were not proper Welsh pit boys. They were the sons of German POW's who had liked the area and stayed behind after the war. That is how proud, strong and solid that culture was.

You could also visit the Big Pit museum, where you can go down an actual coal mine: *http://www.museumwales.ac.uk/en/bigpit/*.

I remember my Aunty's kitchen. She was my father's mother's elder sister. It was always warm, even uncomfortably hot, because the miners got some of their pay in kind; a free coal allowance. It seemed pretty generous. You saw it tipped in heaps along the street. There was a big kettle sitting singing on the range. There were often various family members, from brothers and sisters as far out as second cousins, sitting drinking tea and being told what to do. No-one argued. She was the family matriarch.

The other great thing in the Valley's was rugby. The great Barry John went to the same local school that, years earlier, my father had gone to. There used to be a hysterically funny story in the family of how they had somehow managed to get five tickets for the international at Twickenham. Such tickets were very hard to come by. This being before the days of mass car ownership, the trains being too expensive, and the coach, naturally, being booked out, they all set off for London on Uncle Iorwerth's coal lorry, up the A40 (no motorways in those days), in February, with the ones on the back of the lorry in the freezing wind huddled under piles of empty sacks, changing places with the ones crammed into the cab from time to time. They had a grand time at the game (Wales won), then set off for central London to celebrate. Going round Piccadilly Circus, the lorry broke down and looked like causing a huge traffic jam. But at that point, a Western Welsh bus, well off the route for Victoria Coach Station (probably not by accident) turned up, someone in the bus recognised a cousin on the lorry, everyone piled out to push the lorry to the pavement and help them sort it out. They then all went off to celebrate together. The policeman who arrived to investigate the obstruction was London Welsh and someone else's cousin, so that was all right. Iorwerth and Co. got back to Pontyberem early next day rather the worse for wear, having driven through the freezing night, and went back to work.

Have you ever seen Piccadilly Circus after Wales have won at Twickenham? You really ought to, at least once. It was at Piccadilly Circus that a man in a full head-to-toe Red Dragon costume was arrested for being drunk and disorderly. The following Monday he appeared in court, still in costume, apologised to the Magistrate, saying he had misbehaved because his B&B had fed him scrambled eggs instead of coal, which had upset his stomach.

The reason I still remember the story of Iorwerth's foray to the big city over 50 years later is that I heard it more than once. The reason I heard it more than once was that it was the only story of its kind. Later, through the 1960s and 70s, face-workers in the pits began to make really good money, and even to take holidays abroad; but before then, you might very probably be born, grow up, live, work, become old and die, all in the same valley. Military service 1939–45 was an eye-opener for many, who served all over the world. But coal-mining was vital war work, a reserved occupation, so many did not go. It was a strong culture, tight, tough, proud and intensely loyal to its own; but rather narrow and not especially outward-looking. Even people from the next valley were looked on as a bit odd. The rest of the world didn't really exist at all.

Llanelli, just a few miles away, was also a strong, tight, working class town, but based on a different industry. Llanelli made tinplate. They were proud of it. This was special steel, not the common mild steel churned out in huge quantities in other steelworks. My mother's family came from Llanelli. It, too, was intensely industrial. Railway tracks ran through the streets.

Several times a day, a little engine would come puffing through the town, hauling loads from one works to another. It even had its own cartoon series in the local paper; helping old ladies carry their shopping home, or chasing an unpopular Mayor down the street.

To make tinplate, you take an ingot of steel, heat it until it is a nice yellow-orange, by which point it is quite squashy. You pass it through a series of rollers so that it is squished out into a thin sheet. Then you plate it with best Cornish tin. Before plastics arrived in a big way, tinplate was used for everything from food containers to toys.

You may need an extremely long set of rollers. The rollers in the Llanwern steelworks in Newport are housed in a building almost three miles long; one of the biggest buildings in Britain. If you did not have three miles to play with, you made repeated passes through the same set of rollers. My mother said one of the great class acts in Llanelli, which they used to go and watch, was to see the workmen turning the rolled steel and feeding it back. There was no automated machinery in the 1930s. Imagine; this large sharp-edged piece of spitting orange-hot steel is approaching you down the roller-path at about ten miles an hour.

As it shoots out the end, you catch it in a pair of long-handled tongs, flip it back on itself (it is hot enough to be quite floppy), and feed it back in. It was a bravura performance. If the men had an audience of people, they used to play up to them.

You had just better not miss. If it hits you square-on, it will definitely cut you in half. You may not even bleed to death. The heat will cauterise the wound instantly. Or maybe it will just slice a goodly chunk of you off. Grotesquely mutilated men were not uncommon in the steel towns of that era, or even later. When a friend went to university in Sheffield in the 1960s, he commented how many there were.

In the 1920s and 30s, South Wales had virtually no indigenous middle class. There were a few very small local shops, but for most people, either you were working class or you were English. Being working class meant hard, unremitting, low-paid, dangerous physical work until you were too worn out to go on. If some nasty accident didn't get you, some unpleasant industrial disease probably would. Decent levels of pay and reasonable attention to workers' safety didn't come in until nationalisation, post-WW2. Before then, if you wanted a better life than that, you had to get up and out.

Apart from a few wild talents like Johnny Owen the great boxer, or Shirley Bassey (who grew up in Cardiff's Tiger Bay), the best way out was education. This would throw huge strains on a family's finances. In those days, there were no student grants, not even loans. You paid through the nose. University College Swansea originally consisted of four huts. It was designed to be a shoestring university providing decent intellectual standards at bare minimum of cost. But fees still had to be paid.

The vital question was: how long could the family support the load on their finances? Even if their youngster was bright, and won competitive scholarships, it would still be a considerable strain. The obvious answer was to keep it as short as they could. My grandfather trained as an architect. Unfortunately, the training was seven years. There was a catastrophe in the family finances just before he was due to take his articles. He never qualified. He made his living as a self-employed builder, albeit better trained than most. My parents both played safe and became teachers – a much shorter training.

Thomas Penry Evans became a doctor. Only the very ambitious chose that. The training was seven years. Some parts were expensive. Even though his father, a tin shearer, was a skilled worker, not a common labourer, the strain on the family finances must have been enormous. Thomas Penry Evans was an extremely determined, ruthlessly ambitious, social climber. Given his circumstances, he had to be. If he wasn't, he would never have succeeded. Accounts of him emphasise how strong-willed he was. He had to be. To be fair, while ambition was one of his chief motivations, it was probably not the only one. He had served in a machine-gun unit in the Great War. He was probably attracted to the idea of a career in which he could be saving lives rather than taking them. He qualified in 1925 or 26. He must have begun as soon as he demobbed.

So much for "Merl" and the culture which produced him. What about his wife? Dion Fortune was born Violet Mary Firth. Although she was born in Llandudno, in North Wales ("up in the Gog," as we say in South Wales), her family was from Yorkshire. They were well known in the steel towns of South Wales. The Firths did not work in steelworks – they owned them. For a tin shearer's son to marry one of "THE Firths", as Penry Evans' father used to say, was a huge step up in the world. With class divisions much sharper than today, it would have been almost unimaginable. It did not matter how powerful, capable or magnetic someone born in the "lower orders" might be. Such unions very seldom happened. Dion Fortune was a very brave lady, ready to make a marriage that flew in the face of convention.

To digress, in the nineteenth century, Firth Steels specialised in armaments. It is possible they made the large black-powder rifled muzzle-loaders the Sea Priestess' fort was originally armed with. It is a perfectly real fort, not hard to find, open for visits, well-preserved and completely identifiable. Dion Fortune gives a faithful detailed description of the fort and the surrounding topography in her novel.

No doubt Dion and Penry Evans met through a common interest in magic. It also seems clear he made the very most of what this opportunity gave him. Alan Richardson suggests that he did not marry her simply to "get ahead", because he stayed with her for twelve years. I beg to differ. There is no record that he lived off her money. That seems fairly unlikely. A doctor's pay was not bad. Even though she came from a rich family, she does not seem to have inherited a large chunk of the family fortune. But it is absolutely certain Dion Fortune brought him respectability, a semi-Anglicised identity, and above all contacts and an entrée into the networks of the English upper middle class. She had medical training, so would have had contacts in precisely the areas which would do him the most good. She could introduce him to the right people, open doors for him, smooth the path for him.

If he was seen as socially awkward, with the wrong background and the wrong accent, many influential people would still open their doors to him, for the sake of his wife, who was one of their own. Without her, no matter how good he was as a doctor, he would almost certainly have been frozen out. The best he could have hoped for was not a career, but a life spent in a series of junior posts. In *The Sea Lure*, Dion Fortune's protagonist, Dr Rhodes, refers derisively to being "unable to evade an invitation to spend the evening with an old fellow-student who since the war had held the uninspiring post of medical officer at a poor law institution, a post for which I should say he was admirably fitted."

This was not for Penry Evans. He had a driving ambition and a career to develop. In the 1930s, with jobs hard to come by, if you applied for a job in England from a Welsh address, your job application almost automatically went in the bin unread. Many Welsh people used their cousins among the London Welsh as accommodation addresses for that reason. They tend to cluster around Paddington and Clapham Junction, both great stations with good connections to Wales. Thomas Penry Evans went one better. He moved to London as soon as he qualified, to a bedsit in Queensborough Terrace, less than half a mile from Paddington, squarely in London Welsh territory. He got a job in Charing Cross Hospital as House Surgeon and Medical Registrar in 1926. He wasted no time, marrying Dion the next year.

Over the years, his career progressed through the posts of Tubercular Officer for East Ham, to becoming Medical Officer for a sanatorium in Hampshire. This seems not to have suited him, so he returned to the post of Tubercular Officer, this time for a much wider area, including Southwark, Slough and south-eastern Buckinghamshire. Although he never returned to the Valleys to put his medical skills at the disposal of the communities that had given him his start in life, as many idealistic young doctors did, he seems to have had some shreds of a social conscience left. TB is a disease of the poor. Neither East Ham nor Southwark were rich areas. He obviously did not see himself in a fashionable Mayfair practice, catering to the imaginary ailments of the rich and pampered.

However, while he was working in the public service sector of medicine, he was very much up the prestige end. Until the destruction of the Greater London Council in 1986, London public services had a high reputation among insiders. They were bigger and more efficient, often had extra powers through private Acts of Parliament, and were innovative and cutting edge. If you wanted to progress your career, they were the place to be.

So, would an ambitious working class Llanelli lad have been able to progress his career without his upper-middle class English wife to make introductions, open doors and smooth the path for him? Hardly. Remember, she was also medically qualified and therefore had access to a wide range of useful contacts. Without her, he would almost certainly not have got as far. Then, when he was responsible for a wide area of the southeast, his career was well established, he had established an independent professional reputation and no doubt a file of contacts of his own, he left her.

I think she got very ruthlessly used. Poor Dion. After having the courage to defy convention to make a marriage with a dynamic man who was not only her husband but her magical partner, it came to this. Poor Thomas Penry Evans, too. If he seems not to have been a very nice person, remember what his choices were. Either to claw his way as far up as he could, doing whatever was necessary to get there, or to spend his life flipping lengths of hot steel until he missed one and died or was crippled, or perhaps working underground until the dust got him.

This is why I am so often shocked at today's extremely individualistic society in which selfishness and "grab it while you can any way you can" have been re-branded as virtues. The code-word is "aspiration". This sanitises something quite unpleasant. If people abandon the attempt to create a humane world, by working together collectively, as they very largely seem to have done, we will be forced back into a society in which people are routinely forced to make terrible and very ugly choices. People will once again be forced to exploit and betray each other at the most basic and personal level, if they want to do any better materially than simply survive. What price progress?

Occultic World of Alan Moore

ETHAN DOYLE WHITE

Alan Moore is one of the most important British writers of the last 50 years. His name should rightfully sit alongside those of J.K. Rowling, Philip Pullman and Terry Pratchett. However, mention his name to almost anyone in a bookstore and you will see a blank look come across their face. The reason? Moore likes it that way. He has been somewhat of a recluse, shying away from the limelight, preferring to stay within the borders of his hometown, Northampton – an industrial town in central England – for the past 20 years.

Another reason for his partial obscurity is because whilst he is primarily a fiction author, novels are not his typical medium; that is to say conventional novels are not his typical medium. He has, in fact, been perhaps the most influential writer in the graphic novel (or comic book) medium that Britain has ever seen. His most notable works are milestones in the industry and include *Watchmen* (a work that psychologically deconstructed what it meant to be a superhero), and *V for Vendetta*, which told the tale of a desperate struggle between a fascist government and a violent anarchist committing acts of terrorism.

However, it is not his work that I am so interested in, but rather it is him. For he is a modern day occultic magician, and worships the ancient Pagan snake deity Glycon. He looks the part too, with his long Gandalf-like beard, jet black clothing and heavy silver rings on every finger.

Moore grew up in a working class area of Northampton, becoming involved with the Arts Lad (a hippy-like group of freethinkers) after getting expelled from school for dealing LSD in 1969. He then began his life as a comics writer (initially he was also an illustrator, but he soon gave that up). His big break came in the 1980s when he began working for the American DC Comics company, writing stories about big-name superheroes such as *Batman*, *Superman* and *Swamp Thing*, and eventually moving on to writing *Watchmen*, the great success of his career. Ever since then, he has wandered in and out of the comics mainstream with various projects, several of which have revolved around his magical beliefs.

It was on his 40th birthday in 1993 that Moore suddenly announced to the world that he had become a magician (an occultic magician, not the rabbit-in-a-hat illusionist kind), something he describes with his usual wit as being far more interesting than simply having a mid-life crisis.

His choice of transformation from writer to magician was an obvious choice for him. Moore equates magic with art – whether that be drama, painting, or writing. The reason for this is that they are all designed to change people's consciousness, and this, he says, is the true essence of magic. In today's modern culture, they are seen merely as forms of entertainment, but he asserts that they are virtually interchangeable with the magic of shamans and magicians. He notes that magicians cast "spells" and have grimoires (Old French for "grammar") – a clear link for him between magic and the written word. According to Moore, advertising is also a new kind of magic, it influences thousands of people to all think the same thing, often at the same time, shaping their consciousness to buy something or think a certain way.

Moore's works are brimming with creatures from the imagination, but he, somewhat surprisingly to many people, considers them all to be entirely real. For him, demons and other such mythical beings are real within our minds and that is just as important as things that have an external "real" existence. His magical understanding largely revolves around the "mind space" – a place where the imagination is real, within our minds, which we can all access. He describes it as a place where every major philosophy, from Marxism to the Judaeo-Christian tradition, form continents. We can use maps such as the tarot or Kabbalic tree of life to explore this mind space. The creatures in the mind space have just the same ability to terrify or excite us as anything in the external world, and therefore become very "real" to us.

Moore is a big believer in following the Kabbalic tree of life, even making it a key plot device in his comic series, *Promethea*. The Kabbalah is a set of ancient mystical Jewish teachings (that were adopted into occultic Hermetic philosophies) designed to help followers understand God; and the tree of life contains ten sephiroth, each of which depict an emanation of the true Godhead, such as chesed (loving kindness) and din (judgement). The Kabbalic tree of life has long been an important belief among occult circles and only recently has been associated with the controversial Kabbalah Centre. For Moore, and many other occultists, the sephiroth are very similar to the many different Pagan gods and goddesses, each of which are an emanation of the pantheistic supreme Godhead (equivalent to the Wiccan Dryghten (Old English term for The Lord) or the Hindu Brahman).

Whilst declaring himself a magician, Moore also adopted Glycon as his personal deity. Glycon was the god of an ancient Pagan cult that spread throughout the Roman Empire in the second century CE, founded by the prophet Alexander of Abonutichus. The god Glycon itself was a snake with long blond hair who, according to Alexander, hatched out of a giant egg that he had found. Glycon was a god of fertility whose worship was centred around the fishing town of Ionopolis (in modern Turkey). Even at the time, the cult was a figure of fun, with Alexander's contemporary, the writer Lucian of Samosata (who was responsible for the satirical *True History*) even going so far as to claim that the deity was nothing more than a glove puppet, and that Alexander was a fraud. The very fact that Glycon was probably one big hoax was enough to convince Moore to devote himself to the scaly lord, for, as Moore maintains, the imagination is just as real as reality.

Moore has written various comics based around his occultic Pagan beliefs, the most obvious being the *Promethea* series (1999 to 2005). In the series, a young Pagan girl who's father has been murdered by Christian monks in fifth century Alexandria is rescued by the gods Hermes and Thoth and raised to become the goddess Promethea. She is later incarnated into the body of teenager Sophie Bangs in the year 1999, where she goes on to explore the Immateria (a realm that is obviously meant to be Moore's mind space) and then the Kabbalic tree of life. Along the way, she meets such characters as the ancient Greek god Apollo, Elizabethan occultist John Dee, and the "great beast" himself, Aleister Crowley. The work is somewhat of an occultic textbook in comic form and a very colourful introduction into understanding the Kabbalah.

In the 1990s, Moore wrote a short, four-issue comic book series for Wildstorm Comics entitled, *Voodoo: Dancing in the Dark*, which dealt with an exotic dancer's battles with a demon in New Orleans, and largely featured themes based around Voodoo magic and the Loa (powerful spirits or demi-gods in Louisiana Voodoo).

One of Moore's seminal works is the epic, *From Hell* (upon which the Hollywood film starring Johnny Depp was vaguely based), which is a fictionalized account of the 1888 Whitechapel murders of Jack the Ripper. As its basis, it took Stephen King's theory (a theory Moore does not actually agree with) that Jack the Ripper was a Freemason trying to protect a royal secret, but Moore has enriched it with many occult elements to the story. In the book, Dr William Gull murders and mutilates the five prostitutes as some sort of bizarre ritual to give birth to the twentieth century and protect it from a return to Pagan matriarchy. Of particular note is the fourth chapter, in which Dr Gull takes his coachman on a tour of London to visit five places that have mystical significance, often with ancient Pagan connotations, forming the shape of a giant pentagram across London with Saint Paul's Cathedral in the dead centre.

Many other works by Moore also contain mystical and Pagan elements and themes within them. *Smax* featured twentieth century police officers travelling to a fantasy world inhabited by dwarves, trolls and wizards; whilst *The Courtyard* is set in the Cthulhu Mythos universe originally created by American horror writer H.P. Lovecraft (this universe was assimilated into the magical pantheon by influential occultist Kenneth Graham). Moore's only (non-graphic) novel, *Voice of the Fire*, takes a mystical look at the history of Northampton, and how everything from the year 4,000 BCE to the present day is interconnected.

Soon after coming out as a magician, Moore formed an occultic group along with musicians Tim Perkins and David J (the bassist of goth rock band Bauhaus), giving it the bizarrely comical name of "The Moon and Serpent Grand Egyptian Theatre of Marvels." They have performed various public séances, with J and Perkins providing music and Moore offering up speech after speech of mysterious yet informative verse. The group's self-titled debut séance was held in 1994 and explored the mystical aspects of London, examining such things as the ancient Temple of Diana that, according to legend, once stood where St Paul's Cathedral is now. Since then, four more have been performed and released on CD: *The Birth Caul* (where the human life cycle is used to explore ideas of consciousness), *The Highbury Working* (which explored the Highbury area of London and its association with Aleister Crowley), *Snakes and Ladders* (performed at a meeting of the Hermetic Order of the Golden Dawn), and *Angel Passage* (which looked at the life of mystic William Blake). Moore and his group are issuing an upcoming book entitled, *The Moon and Serpent Bumper Book of Magic*, which looks set to be the first occult textbook ever to offer "endless necromantic fun for all the family!"

I owe Moore a debt of gratitude, for not only have his works given me hours of splendid reading entertainment, but he has also inspired me to pick up the pen and begin my own writing career. His occult and Pagan knowledge coupled with his extraordinary writing talent have helped to make him one of the great eccentrics of his age, and, most importantly, he has helped to open the gateway into the magical real of the mind space for me, and many others like me, allowing the many wonders (including the odd snake god) to escape.

Of Trolls, Terrorists and Petty Tyrants

JULIAN VAYNE

"My benefactor used to say that a warrior who stumbles on a petty tyrant is a lucky one."

– Don Juan.

It has to be said; some people are a right pain in the arse (or 'ass' if you prefer). We could be all gently liberal and thoughtful and talk about the difficulties we might experience with others as being about problems of relationship – the issues is 'between us' and not necessarily the fault of either party. However, sometimes we come across someone in our lives who, for us, fits into the role that Carlos Castaneda (or rather his literary creation, Don Juan) described as a 'petty tyrant'. Such a person might be a bitter ex-partner, a manipulative co-worker, a playground bully, or (thanks to the internet) a tedious online troll (actually there are various classes of petty tyrant according to Carlos and indeed the term does appear in the work of other theorists).

According to Castaneda, the petty tyrant, although clearly irritating (and even potentially threatening in cases where they wield temporal power), can act as a goad to the progress of the 'impeccable warrior'. "A petty tyrant is a tormentor. Someone who either holds the power of life and death over warriors, or simply annoys them to distraction." Within his model, Castaneda suggests that the petty tyrant is an adversary who, if handled correctly, can actually empower the person whom the petty tyrant is attempting to victimise.

Typically, someone who finds themselves in a petty tyrant role is stuck in a situation, locked into a looping Groundhog Day of their own bitterness. In that respect, they deserve our compassion (if not our appreciation). What they typically lack is any ability to think outside of their own reality tunnel (as Leary and Wilson would put it), and one critical diagnostic feature is their lack of a sense of humour (especially the ability to laugh at oneself). This is hardly surprising given the vital role that humour plays in broadening our perspectives and shaking up entrenched ways of thinking.

Castaneda writes:

> *"The mistake average men make in confronting petty tyrants is not to have a strategy to fall back on; the fatal flaw is that average men take themselves too seriously; their actions and feelings, as well as those of the petty tyrants, are all-important. Warriors, on the other hand, not only have a well-thought-out strategy, but are free from self-importance. What restrains their self-importance is that they have understood that reality is an interpretation we make … Petty tyrants take themselves with deadly seriousness while warriors do not."*

So a sense of humour is an essential attribute when we find ourselves in these situations, including practices that challenge our own sense of self-importance. Our interpretation of reality may well be that our petty tyrant is doing any number of vile things to us, but if we step aside from our own self-importance (and our sense of being got-at) we can notice how other people are actually reacting to the antics of our foe. If our adversary is just another hopping-bonkers voice on the internet (for example), we can be sure that other intelligent people will judge their buffoonery with the scorn it deserves.

Castaneda is not the only person to explore the benefits that can be found in our dealings with difficult people and situations.

Shakespeare makes the same point, speaking through the character of Duke Senior in *As You Like It*:

> *"Sweet are the uses of adversity*
> *which like the toad ugly and venomous*
> *wears yet a precious jewel in his head."*

Of course, the petty tyrant, as minor league irritation (the first-world problem of internet trolling, for example) is worlds away from the potentially life-threatening situations where people are living under actual tyranny. Whether it is dressed in the glossy veneer of oh-so-reasonable military-industrial capitalism, or pro-Medievalist Muslim fundamentalism, we can find ourselves in situations where the tyrant swells to become a fully-fledged monster; in control of money, weapons and information sources. Luckily the petty tyrants most of us encounter are a toothless version of these much more serious foes. Even so, those same strategies that Castaneda outlines can help – don't become stuck in our own self-importance, use humour, be patient, realise that others also think as we do.

Castaneda counsels us:

> *"To tune the spirit when someone is trampling on you is called 'control'. Instead of feeling sorry for himself, a warrior immediately goes to work mapping the petty tyrant's strong points, his weaknesses, his quirks of behaviour."*

Mapping the behaviour of petty tyrants is generally pretty simple because they are typically stuck in that repetitive rut mentioned above. They act more like automata because their obsessive behaviours have eaten up their creative humanity. Watch them as they indulge in the same attempts to goad and upset again and again and again. Any apparent change in their behaviour tends to be a minor variation on the same theme.

Even in extreme cases, such as the release of images by the Islamic State of executions and the smashing of artworks, there is a simplistic (albeit horrific) repetition in these calculated attempts to goad and distress the enemy. As with most bullies, the hope is to get a reaction, which is why one of the best ways to respond to these terrible films is not to click 'play'. Given the fact that human neurology is optimised to remember distressing stuff, it's unsurprising that there is a part of us that wants to watch that car crash, or view the burning of a Jordanian pilot. In the lesser case of the petty tyrant, we may want to ask: "what is so-and-so saying about me now?" but again the best course of action is to rise above it. Let those attempts to gain attention fall on stony ground. This is not the same as completely ignoring what is going on (we may know, for example, that the distressing material placed online by terror groups and deranged keyboard warriors exists), but this is about not falling into a reactive trap; into an agenda set by the terrorist or the troll.

The petty tyrant gives us a fabulous opportunity to practice our Tonglen Meditation. This practice has various benefits. Within the context of the technique (which, if you're not familiar with it, basically consists of sending nice thoughts to ourselves and then everyone in the world, including our enemies), we are actively working for the liberation from suffering of our petty tyrant. Psychologically, we're ensuring that when we battle with monsters, as Nietzsche puts it, we don't become monsters ourselves; we strengthen our impeccability and are more likely to put ourselves into a mindset suitable to gather a community of support and resistance around us. In addition, we're actively using the upset that our petty tyrant wills against us as fuel for our own spiritual illumination and liberation. By giving thanks for our ability to see the tyrant, petty or otherwise, as a chance for growth rather than a reason for regret, we strengthen our own psyche.

As they say on the internet: win!

Sacred Sites – Islay and the Paps of Jura

CHERYL STRAFFON

Loch Finnigan was the centre of power of the whole of the Inner Hebrides and the Kintyre peninsula. From the twelfth to the sixteenth century, the Lords of the Isles were formally installed here in their high positions of power. In order to rule, however, they had to gain their power by placing their foot on a sacred stone in a hollow in the rock which was in the shape of a foot. A similar custom is known about elsewhere, such as at Dunadd on the Mull of Kintyre, at Halkirk in Caithness, at South Ronaldsway on Orkney and at Clickhimin on Shetland, and may be a continuation of a pre-Christian custom whereby the ruler of the tribe could only obtain his right to rule by gaining authority from the Goddess of the Land, Sovereignity. On Islay, this stone stood on the islet of Eilean Mor in Loch Finnigan (NR 388 680) and was said to be the burial place of the queens and children of the Lords of the Isles. Excavations and geophysical surveys by the Time Team here in 1994 have shown that a natural mound, Cnoc Seavida, near to the shore of the Loch, contained a stone chamber that may have been a Neolithic barrow into which the bones of an animal were ritually deposited. From this mound, a single standing stone about 5ft high (NR 392 685) was aligned to the rounded hills of the Paps, and, despite the intervention of the Visitor Centre, can still be seen today. In fact, the stone (which was originally part of a stone row) actually stands in the cleavage of the Paps when viewed from the mound. Clearly, the memory of the sacredness of this place in Neolithic times was continued into the historic period when it became the centre of power for the Inner Hebrides.

Sometimes, memory of the goddess is held in the names of places, and another loch on Islay retains that association. Loch Conailbhe (NR 215 600) actually means "Loch of the Goddess" and lies equidistant between two standing stones (NR 224 605 & NR 211 593). Perhaps, like Loch Finnigan, this too was a sacred loch in ancient times, the memory of which only remains in the name.

On Jura, the Paps themselves are often hidden from lower ground on the island but the stones that do seem to be aligned to the Paps include two near to Knockrome, nowadays rather insignificant because they have sunk into the peat, but in fact noted in the 1970s as being 7ft high.[10] These two stones seem each to point to one of the two Paps, the westerly stone (NR 547 715) being shaped to mirror the slope of the eastern Pap; and the easterly stone (NR 551 715) being aligned to the westerly Pap. What makes this site even more fascinating is that in the opposite direction an observer would see Eilean Bhride offshore, a double-hilled islet named after the Celtic Goddess/Saint Bride. At this place, island, standing stones and Paps seem all to be connected and in significant relationship.

Although it can be recognised that many of the standing stones on Islay & Jura were deliberately aligned to the Paps of Jura, what of those that seem to have been put up in places where the Paps were not visible? It may well be that the connection to the Mother Goddess in the land was such an important part of megalithic culture that even in those places where the Paps themselves were not visible, the local tribes replicated the effects of the alignments in the hills and mounds surrounding their sacred sites. For example, the standing stone of Knockdon near Loch Skerrois on Islay (NR 336 642), from which the Paps are

10   Gordon Wright, *Jura's Heritage* [D.G.B. Wright, 1994].

not visible, instead looks towards a nearby twin hill site, a kind of Paps of Jura in miniature.

Again, in the south of Islay, one of the standing stones to the east of Port Ellen (NR 384 466) stands on a prominent knoll and aligns perfectly to the nearby breast-shaped hill of Borraichill Mor. This stone is particularly interesting because later, in the early Christian period, a chapel was built here called Kilbride, but dedicated to St. Lasar, an obscure sixth century female saint who was doubtless an avatar of the Goddess/Saint Bride. Even her feast day Feb 1st (the old Celtic Imbolc festival) was the same. She was also known in Ireland as Saint Lasair, one of three sisters, all of whom were localised in an area in Co. Cork/Kerry near to the Paps of Anu, the Irish equivalent of the Paps of Jura. Clearly, this particular saint is directly associated with sites that are close to representations of the breasts of the Mother Goddess. What is also interesting is that this standing stone, the chapel of Kilbride and a chapel on the islet of Texa about a mile offshore are all in a direct alignment, a situation paralleling the one on Jura mentioned above. There is even another Eilean Bhride islet near to Texa offshore! Perhaps these two early Christian chapels stand on sites of pre-Christian significance, sites that were associated with the Earth Goddess and which became Christianised into holy places of Lasair/Bride.

On Jura, many of the standing stones seem to be aligned to significant hills on Islay, a mirror image of the Islay-Paps of Jura syndrome. For example, the standing stone Camus-an-Stac (NR 455 647) is, according to Professor Alexander Thom, aligned to the summit of Sgorr Nam Faoileann on Islay (compass bearing 213° 40') which would have marked the midwinter solstice sunset in about 1700 BCE. Thom also worked out a moon alignment for this site, where the minimum moonset would have been behind the hill Beinn Bheigeir on Islay (compass bearing 199°). The hill visible between the two may also have been of significance, as its name that has come down to us is Beinna Callich, the hill of the Calleach.

The final site that needs examining is the only major stone circle site on Islay at Cultoon (NR 196 570). Here three stones stand out of an original fifteen (many are recumbent). It has been calculated that the site would have formed an accurate ellipse with the long axis aligned NE–SW directly in line with Slieve Snaght in Co. Donegal in Ireland, which is visible from Cultoon on a clear day. This is very close to the position where the sun would have set on midwinter day in 1800 BCE, and is therefore another significant alignment to a holy hill top. It has been suggested that because pits were prepared for many of the stones but the stones never erected, the circle proved to be unworkable or ineffective and was therefore abandoned. However, a close examination of the circle suggests another possibility. Although the Paps of Jura are not visible from the site, it sits in a natural amphitheatre, surrounded by about a dozen distinctive hills. One of these is a noticeable breast-shaped mound, and the top of the principal upright stone standing in the circle looks towards this mound, with the shape of the top of the stone actually cut into a representation of the Paps of Jura themselves. This may be fortuitous but it is certainly a curious "coincidence". The other stones in the circle that were never placed upright seem in their turn to mirror the particular shape of the hill to which they align when viewed from the centre of the circle. This may all have been intended by the circle's builders, or it may not, but it is certainly something worth serious consideration.

So, in conclusion it seems that the Paps of Jura were a focal point for a number of prehistoric monuments in the surrounding area of the mainland and the islands of Islay and Jura. This was manifested in the alignment of the stones to the Paps, sometimes at significant astronomical times, and sometimes in the shapes and positions of the stones themselves. Where the Paps were not visible, similar nearby breast-shaped hills were chosen. The whole terrain of standing stones, mounds and circles, all in relationship to the breasts of the hills of the Earth Goddess, forms a fascinating ritualistic prehistoric landscape.

Satanism for Today

HUGO L'ESTRANGE AKA
RAMSEY DUKES

This article arose from the publicity given to Satanism by the hilarious 'Satan Sting' trial of 1986. In particular, it was *The Guardian* which had the distinction of being the only newspaper to write a fairly sensible article on the subject, so Hugo decided that they should be offered the chance to publish an article by a genuine Satanist. Alas, the result proved too steamy for what turned out to be their religious columns.

There is a problem in trying to present the Satanist's case. It is that as soon as I write anything that sounds at all reasonable, or agreeable, or even endearing, my words are liable to be dismissed as 'not real Satanism.' Why? 'Because Satanism is totally evil.'

There is an analogy: a strong case could be made to prove that President Reagan is not a Christian: he is not meek and mild, he shows no sign of turning the other cheek, nor of renouncing worldly wealth ... On the other hand HE considers himself to be a Christian, and his supporters would largely agree. So, at the practical level of this article, I go along with his belief.

In return I do not expect when I show signs of flagging from my heavy round of blasphemy and blood sacrifice to be told that I am therefore not a 'real Satanist'. Let him who is without merit throw the first raspberry.

The subject of Satanism is surrounded with veils of illusion. Removing those veils one by one, we do seem to approach a more credible core. The first veil is the idea, held by Christian fanatics and popular journalists, that the only alternative to science or religion is a thing called 'black magick'.

The second veil embodies the more useful notion that there is also something called 'white magick'. White magick is magick employed for purposes of good, black magick is magick employed for purposes of evil.

Anyone of open mind who has experience of white magicians will surely agree that we are moving in the direction of truth, relative to the last veil.

The third veil defines a continuum between these poles: arguing that there are many shades of magick, depending upon the practitioner's purity of intent and relative selflessness. Satanism is the embodiment of the extreme black end of this 'spectrum'. Sometimes this continuum is seen as a slippery slope leading down to Satanism, analogous to the view that the political left is a slippery slope which plunges unavoidably into ultimate communism.

The last idea is a reasonable day-to-day belief (whether in its magical or political form). With it one can win friends and influence people, write acceptable articles, earn a living … But it has its limitations for the experienced magician who will, one day, wake up and ask, 'who the hell actually does magick for the purposes of evil?'

The only people likely to dedicate themselves to absolute evil would be the odd artist or pimply adolescent going through a decadent crisis. Far from seeing that minority as a Great Cosmic Threat, I feel quite affectionate towards them, love them for their fleeting efforts to add a little colour to our lives. If black magick is a tool of absolute evil, it is neither prevalent nor dangerous.

Removing the next veil, we recognize that pure evil is virtually impotent. All really dangerous and vicious acts are dedicated not to pure evil, but to over-refined notions of good. If Adolf Hitler had initially announced a movement dedicated to pure evil, or even to providing an outlet for man's common nastiness, he would have remained a harmless crank. Instead, the exoteric aims were to revive Germany, to create a new 'order', and to be safe from the evils of communism – all very good, and all very similar to the aims of present day government.

So black magick, if it is indeed a powerful and dangerous alternative to white magick, must mean something other than magick done for evil purposes.

Removing the next veil we see a different polarity, one that really does reflect a vital distinction. Although there are few who openly admit to black magick, those who do, and those most likely to be labelled 'black' by knowledgeable persons, are not so much those people working for evil, as those who work with evil. The whitest magicians are extremely unwilling to do anything but banish demons and evil forces, while black magicians will acknowledge, respect and even risk the dangers of working with such forces.

I will give a psychological example. A university student has a nervous break- down, is torn apart by inner violence. He is directed to the psychiatrist who banishes this demon with the 'sword of analysis'. This is white magick: it frees the student to return to his work, get a good degree, and carve a successful career. After twenty years of success, however, there is a lingering malaise. He feels poisonously guilty, because nothing obvious is actually wrong – it is all just a little pointless. He now goes to a different more expensive type of analyst, who reveals that the demon banished was in fact a valid part of his make-up, and when it departed it took life's magick with it. The task now is a dangerous one, it is to make an inner journey to renew contact with that now deeply incarcerated demon and attempt to assimilate or redeem it in order to restore the fullness of life. This is black magick (perhaps that's why it costs more!).

Don't say it must be white magick because the purpose is good: to approach such demons as a righteous crusader is unwise, just as (presumably) the lion tamer is not one who sets out to destroy a lion's basic nature. The aim is better called 'wholeness' than 'good'.

White magick does an excellent job but, in these terms, it does not do the whole job. Those who risk the mucky bits left over can call themselves black magicians, but not in public.

Psychological examples don't suit everyone, so I'll balance it with a simplified political one. Someone organizes an atrocity to express their anger. The horror of this act catches the imagination of a slightly bored public and it is named 'terrorism'. Publicity validates the act, and in a few years you have a movement. This process is called 'evocation' of a demon, the demon of terrorism.

The demon begins to feed on the social equivalent of psychic energy, but it remains out there rather than a real danger. Then comes a new development: people in no real danger begin to feel threatened, and personally involved in the 'fight' against terrorism. This is called 'possession by the demon', because these people will forget that a demon is a discarnate entity, and direct their attack against a (typically) human target. Bombs are dropped on the Libyan people in an attempt to destroy an abstract principle. The demon which causes men to express violence by politically aimed violence is now exultantly pulling the trigger; those who most loudly oppose 'terrorism' have become terrorists, and denounce as weak those with stronger and more resistant minds!

The white magician would banish an evil demon; the black would make a pact with it. Be warned, accounts of black magick pacts can cause offence.

A relationship is made with the demon, a sort of understanding, but less the analytical 'banishing' approach of white magick. Appreciate what fun the initial plans of a terrorist attack could be. Then consider how often early IRA bombs were defused harmlessly after a warning phone call – a procedure seldom adopted by legal governments who underestimate the power of imagined explosions and prefer to kill outright. When an IRA nail bomb first exploded in London, it was heralded as a sign that the terrorists were 'worse than animals'; yet the US

Government used plastic shrapnel in Vietnam because it was too easy to separate metal fragments from human flesh. It begins to look as if terrorism is more gentlemanly than the governments it opposes. And the vast majority of British have suffered more under Thatcherism than from the sum total of terrorist activity. Sympathy for the Devil does not mean identity with the Devil: there is even a sense in which the very horrors of black magick make it safer than white magick.

What happens next is not predictable, for black magick is more anarchic than white. One simply acts from one's new-found perspective. Outwardly, one might act the same as the non-magician: one might bomb Libya. However (and this is where the rationalist abandons us in ridicule and despair), the magician believes that, however similar the outward act, the long-term result will be different. One's aim will be truer, because it will be a human rather than a demonic finger on the trigger.

Satanism, as the extreme of black magick, calls for a relationship with one's ultimate demon. This is likely to be a more general and personal evil than terrorism, but our Christian establishment is helpful in defining such devils. For example, consider a nice, hard-working teenager who never rebels. He develops a horrid repulsion for the loud, brazen bullies who lay all the best girls and then, a few years later, get all the best-paid jobs. To him, Satan is the lord of the world, the flesh and aggression. This possession is confirmed when, as an adult, he finds himself madly in love with another man's wife: the other man is painfully nice, and his wife is a compellingly brazen slut who made all the running. If he is lucky, he awakens to the fact that it is himself that he is hurting; exaggerated guilt comes from identifying with the suffering husband. He begins to notice how the husband is passively exacerbating the situation; the realization that the husband and he are both onto the same kick (possessed by the same devil) is the time for magick. White magick would end the affair, while the Satanist might consider flaunting his sexual triumph before the simpering wimp. This apparently callous act would pay homage to a shared demon through which the Satanist would know how the other person felt: if a hopeless case, the wimp's life would at least be elevated into the sweet masochism of a cosmic tragedy; if not, the crisis could awaken him to freedom. In either case, adultery takes on new pleasures, for one has learned how to relate to humans as well as to demons.

In these examples, I have not managed to define precisely the nature of the relationship with Satan. To expect that in a short article: what is the precise nature of any religious devotion? Nor have I dwelt on the precise ritual forms and prayers, but rather on the principles. The former are so varied and personal that they would only obscure the basic argument. It is also too easy to read one's prejudices into the details of other peoples' religion; the Holy Communion shows ample evidence of being a cannibalistic cult if you look for that evidence.

Nor have I dwelt on blood sacrifice. This is partly due to squeamishness: someday I must do it for my own salvation. Satanic blood sacrifices are sporadic rather than performed on the grand scale.

Personally, though I recognize the need, I feel that the need for large-scale human sacrifice is more the mark of an old and weary religion. There is little doubt that Christian fervour in Ulster is nourished by spilt blood, and that the major human sacrifice at Jonestown has done its job of reversing the decline in church attendance in the USA. Satanism has not been reduced to such extremes.

As a traditional Satanist I despise the Christian Church, but am untypical in that I respect its origins. Christianity and communism are the religions of the underdog; as such they both perform wonders when kept in their place by persecution. But as soon as such religions rise to institutional power, they turn extremely nasty.

The world becomes a wonderfully civilized place when you embrace Satan: for years you have been believing the world 'needs Christian principles because without them men would revert to savagery,' then one day you reject those principles and find, like the humanists, that you do not revert to savagery! Then you realize that anyone who holds such beliefs about mankind has got something pretty nasty pulling the strings at the back of his mind. Having discovered how nice you yourself really are, you want to invite that nastiness to the dance.

To return to the problem with which this article began: the world of Satan is The World. So, I make my judgement not on spiritual principle but on worldly effects. The person who spends an hour each Sunday in church likes to be considered a Christian, even if he spends the other six days being greedy, arrogant, vicious, aggressive and lustful. The Satanist who performs monthly rites which would make *The News of the World* curl up and turn yellow, would similarly like to consider himself a Satanist and would like to be forgiven the other days when he lapses into a twinkle-eyed philanthropist.

One drawback of the Christian despisal of the world and the flesh is that more extreme Christians feel free to exert correspondingly extreme pressures on the body and property of those whose souls they wish to save.

The Magick and Mystery of Maurice/ Margaret Bruce

MELISSA SEIMS

This is the story of the mystery and mischief of a woman perhaps best-known for her exotic perfumes, talismans and mail-order Magick. Her adverts, often later seen alongside the promotion of her animal sanctuary, were found frequently in *Prediction* and other alternative publications over many decades.

She was involved in Magickal matters for well over 50 years. Most will know of her as Margaret Bruce, but she was born Maurice Marks Bruce.

Margaret's is a story of change on one level, but also a story of being a constant; true to herself and her core beliefs – something you will hopefully see for yourself as we enter Margaret Bruce's mail-order world of Magick.

MAURICE MARKS BRUCE

Maurice M. Bruce was born on 31st March, 1926, in Darlington, Durham to Montague Marks Bruce and Eleanor Raper. He was born 11 years after his parents' marriage in 1915 and doesn't appear to have had any siblings, making him an only child. Before Maurice was 10, his parents divorced and both of them subsequently remarried. It appears he may have become estranged from his father, for on Montague's gravestone, located in a Jewish cemetery, there is no mention of him having a son or a daughter, referring only to his second wife, nephews and nieces.

Maurice was expelled from school for having *"unnatural and sinister interests of such a vile nature as to make his further attendance at this school quite intolerable."*

When a little older, he became a frogman and a commando in the Navy. He also seems to have a Royal Air Force service number; though I have been unable to find any further evidence of his time spent with the RAF. After leaving the armed forces, Maurice became a clerk at the Darlington Transport Corporation. He left this job due to wanting to live as a woman and not wishing to cause any embarrassment.

There is a picture of Maurice Bruce, as a young girl, with the subtitle taken from a Thomas Hardy poem of *"When I came back from Lyonesse with magic in my eyes..."* which comes from a 1984 booklet, *Magick*, by [Maurice] Margaret Bruce, produced under her Angel Press imprint. It appears on a page entitled *"Images Within Images"*. She looks to be around 5 or 6 years old, is wearing girl's clothes and has long, somewhat dishevelled hair. Those of you who have had children will know that they can be very strong-willed, which makes one wonder if the choice of girl's clothes and long hair was hers or, perhaps her parents? It doesn't seem to reflect the fashions worn by boys in the early 1930s.

The only thing I can say for certainty is that at this age, Margaret was officially a boy named Maurice.

In 1951, Maurice married the Austrian woman Margarethe Gabriella Schneider; though she typically used the name Gretel. Unfortunately, I haven't been able to find out how or where they met but I understand that Gretel ended up in the UK whilst still a child as a result of having to forcibly leave Austria during the Second World War.

Gretel was once described as dark and attractive, but Charles Clark, who met both the Bruce's, described Gretel to me as somewhat "mannish".

Gerald Gardner, who seems to have first known Maurice in the 1950s, was clearly impressed and referred to him as *"the Magician of the North."* In *Gerald Gardner Witch*, we find the following extract:

> *"There is 'One Magician I know, whom I call the Magician of the North, though I don't say where he is North of.' This man is the grandson of a man skilled in magical ways, and steeped in the traditional lore of the occult. 'But, as so often happens among witches as well, the power seems to have skipped a generation.'"*

In this section, Gardner is referring to a claim made in a 1958 letter to him from Maurice where he tells Gardner that his maternal grandfather was a 9=2 grade in the Stella Matutina (this was a magical order called Morning Star) and also had a connection with the Witch Cult.

Unfortunately, having investigated Maurice's claim, this cannot be substantiated. Maurice's mother's name was Eleanor Raper, and her father's name Alfred Thomas Raper. There are no extant records to indicate that there was ever a Mr Raper in the Golden Dawn or any of its offshoots. Furthermore, claims of being 9=2 are generally considered to be self-delusionary ego-trips. That said, the main place such elevated grade titles were seen was in the Stella Matutina's Hermes temple in Bristol. In 1934, when Israel Regardie joined this temple, he found that many of the original Knowledge Lectures had been *"withdrawn or heavily amended, largely because they were beyond the capacity of the chiefs,"* and found that the chiefs claimed *"extraordinarily exalted"* grades. Alfred T. Raper died in 1935 in Darlington, County Durham, aged 76. Thus, it seems unlikely that he was involved with the Hermes temple.

Despite this questionable connection to senior membership of the Golden Dawn – considered by many to be the equivalent of magical "royalty" – Margaret was actually the second cousin, once removed to Carole Middleton, the mother of Kate Middleton (now the Duchess of Cambridge), mother of Prince George – who follows his grandfather Prince Charles and his father Prince William, as third in line to the British throne.

Returning now to *Gerald Gardner Witch*, the section continues with a story of how, at aged 8, Maurice had turned a small cottage in his parents' garden into a wizard's den and got hold of some magical books including Waite's *Ceremonial Magic* and Barrett's *The Magus and Budge's Egyptian Magic*; inventively borrowing these from the local library under the name of a fictional uncle. He made and consecrated "instruments of the Art" and began making natural perfumes and incense. By the time he was 12, he believed he could influence things magically.

Maurice realised that many natural magical components could be harvested from the wilds around his home. Upon finding that some books gave different names for the same plant and suggested different correspondences, he decided to take a sympathetic magic approach, discovering exactly what an ingredient was wanted for, and then finding something which had that effect. We are told that after much experimenting and nearly killing himself in the process, he finally worked out how to get the desired results.

A somewhat humorous recollection of this near disastrous experience is seen in a 1958 letter to Gardner from Maurice:

> "*The Geomancy Ritual went smoothly until I sprinkled the black poppy and hemlock seeds on the charcoal. The next thing that I knew was that the floor had tilted to an impossible angle and I was lying in a cold sweat and shivering with fear. It was the first time that I had ever heard a colour or noticed that a wall can wear an expression. Fortunately, the incense burned out but it was days before I could look at an article of furniture without noticing that it was looking back at me. I was careful what incense I used after that and kept off the Saturnine Rituals.*"

In another letter to Gardner, we glimpse more of Maurice's nature as he writes:

> *"… I was always asking country people if they had any spells. I was always inclined to be misanthropic because of the ignorant opposition that my interest aroused. I would much rather have met a Dryad or a Nymph than any mortal – bar none and so I was regarded as 'a most unnatural child.' I didn't care because Magic was all that I lived for."*

These early interests went on to prefigure precisely what Maurice became in the 1950s when he established his own magical mail-order supply business which he initially ran from his home at 166 Yarm Road, Darlington in County Durham. He even followed the instructions in *The Book of the Sacred Magic of Abramelin the Mage*, devoting six months to the performance of the Abramelin operation. He prepared his house, complete with a special sanded terrace into which various spirits could be evoked. In later correspondence, Bruce demonstrates a deep understanding of the Abramelin "squares", so we can but presume that the operation was successful.

His wife, Gretel, helped him with this endeavour and they had little interference, for he told Gardner that he *"had no friends and hated all his neighbours."* Such independence and self-sufficiency was core to Maurice and Gretel's beliefs and is evident throughout their life.

In the late 1950s, Maurice was writing articles and an occasional column entitled the "Occult Mail Box" for the alternative fetishist magazine, *London Life*. This publication was infamous for readers' letters about dress fetishes (it was banned by the Irish government in 1932), but also deserves acclaim for the inventiveness of its mastheads in the 1930s and the quality of its reproduction and printing.

Madeline Montalban and her then partner, Nicholas Heron, were also writers for this publication.

Maurice was a one-time good friend of Madeline's and around 1958 she bought a perfume still for him to make his products. They reputedly later fell out over this and some bracelets that Madeline had ordered from Maurice which he had defaulted on.

Bruce also tells us that in 1936, he inherited *"one of the rare 'still-room' perfumeries to survive into the twentieth century,"* As he would only have been 10 at the time, this seems unrelated to the one that Madeline may have bought him.

In a *Prediction* magazine article from 1958, there is an article by Madeline called "Magic You Can Do Yourself". She talks about helping prepare a manuscript of Maurice's for publication and expresses thanks for both his help with her own researches and for making her a special perfume *"she had long needed for a certain experiment."*

Madeline is probably best-known for writing many astrological and tarot articles under various pseudonyms. These were commonly seen in *Prediction* magazine, which started its run in 1936, with Madeline's first article published in 1953. She was also the founder of the Order of the Morning Star. Following the 1958 publication of Charles Cardell's article and advert in *Light*, and Cardell's ire over Gardner's publicity-seeking, there was a parting of ways between the two of them. Cardell then enlisted Olwen Greene (AKA Olive Green) as a willing spy in order to acquire a copy of Gardner's *Book of Shadows*. There was now mischief afoot, and Maurice became a party to it.

Maurice sent Cardell a Copper Bracelet, telling him it that it was very special and unique as it had come from a fifteenth century Madonna. The reality was that it was a copper bracelet that Maurice had made for his wife, Gretel, but she hadn't really liked it. Maurice suggests in a letter to Gardner that he will make him a very similar one so that Gardner can claim that he actually has the true original!

In 1959, Doreen Valiente mentions in her diaries that during her visit with Charles Cardell in 1958, he had produced a copper bracelet with the name "Gretel" on it in Theban Script, and sigils of Venus from the Arbatel and the Heptameron. We can confidently say that this was Gretel Bruce's. The inclusion of Venusian sigils is a nice touch and suggests something of Maurice and Gretel's relationship. Doreen, intrigued, had subsequently written to Edith Woodford-Grimes to say that the bracelet *"is not the same as ours, but bears sufficient resemblance to be worthy of our attention."*

In this same time period, Maurice is engaged in writing to Cardell using the pseudonyms "Trog" or "The Toad" – a creature for which he expressed a fondness. His cards to Cardell would include a picture of a fat ugly toad capturing a fly – undoubtedly depicting what Maurice felt he was doing, with Cardell being symbolised by the fly. This was several years prior to the inflammatory publication of Cardell's 1964 booklet, *Witch*.

Gretel came up with a mischievous suggestion that she and Maurice could start sending phoney relics to Cardell from a fake high priestess with an Austrian address. They even worked out the finer details of how they could do this living, as they were, in County Durham. They suggest to Gardner:

> *"We thought of a sort of curved Virile Member made on the same principle as those tumbling clowns who refuse to lie down. Round the base, in a neat Theban Script, would be engraved the profound observation PENI TENTO NON PENITENTI"* (a tense penis not penitence).

At this same time, Maurice was also sending calculated and deliberately misleading letters to Olive Green/Olwen Greene (witch name Florannis). Olive had now been outed as a "spy" for Cardell and in a show of solidarity with Gardner, Maurice delighted in reporting back to Gardner on his acts of mischief:

> *"She* [Olive] *is a genuine trouble-maker and needs something to occupy her mind (I might think of something). The trouble*

is she knows that I know you [Gardner]. *I mentioned that I had occasional correspondence with you and had seen the museum but in an offhand manner as though I were not particularly interested. I ignored almost everything in her letter and concentrated on giving her vague 'good advice' on how to become an 'Adept'. I told her to ignore all the adverts for occult lodges and insist that Charles Cardell teach her real Magick because 'he is the one person I know who has an honest approach to magic.' ... In fact, my letter was so 'innocent' that it bordered on imbecility."*

Shortly after, in early 1960, Maurice further tells Gardner:

"I have tried to give her [Olive] *the impression that I am a semi-literate farm labourer in order to discourage her from writing. If you do have any communication with her perhaps you could help keep up the illusion."*

Further insight into Maurice's prankish nature can be seen in a letter from him to Gardner where he writes:

"I could send you one of the minor Demons in a bottle. You could exhibit it with a notice saying that if anyone is sceptical, they can open it IN THEIR OWN HOME. You would have to make them sign a form clearing you of all responsibility because the results would be pretty shattering ... If you want this you must not disclose where it was obtained. I could probably fix some publicity for this unique exhibit, and it should attract the Americans. I think it would be better not to allow anyone to open the thing ... In any case, the Demon would materialise from time to time within the bottle."

It is clear that Maurice, at this time, is sending Gardner all sorts of curios for his museum, which included a pressed datura leaf and is generally keeping an eye out for pertinent witchy objects for Gerald at local antique shops. He is also engaged with making wands and Athames for Gardner.

MAURICE BECOMES MARGARET

Around the early 60s, and definitely by 1963, Maurice publicly started using the name Margaret and openly living life as a woman. The first evidence I have found for this would seem to be from the April/May 1963, first issue of *New Dimensions* magazine which contains the article "Making Magick Work" by Margaret Bruce. This must have been a brave move but there is no doubt her strength of character and the support from Gretel put her in good stead. One can't help but wonder how Gretel really took this. It seems she took it very well and publicly supported Maurice by claiming that she decided to change her own name to Gretel at the same time as stated in a May 1966 *The People* news article by reporter Ken Graham. He visited Margaret and Gretel at their home on Yarm Road and recounts his recollections:

> *"I was received – by appointment – by the dark and attractive Mrs. Greta Bruce. She used to be Margrethe, but when Maurice became Margaret, they decided to change her name to Greta, to avoid confusion. 'Now we live together more as sisters,' Greta said … 'It is very difficult for Margaret. People have told me I should have the marriage annulled but why should I? She needed me more through this change and I have stuck by her.'"*

Putting to one side the likely reporter's mistake of referring to Gretel as "Greta", this account suggests that perhaps, behind closed doors, Maurice had been Margaret for a while. We do know that Margarethe was using the name Gretel several years earlier, as seen in the late 1950s letters between Maurice and Gardner which are signed from "Maurice and Gretel".

Margaret rarely mentions or even alludes to Gretel in her more public writings, suggesting Margaret had a firm distinction between her public and personal life. Regardless, Gretel certainly remained by Margaret's side.

In the same 1966 article, we also have a description of Margaret on that day as *"tall, dressed in a high-necked cocktail dress, nylons and wearing charm bracelets and rings."* She offers the reporter her *"nail-varnished hand"* and makes a joke about how with a 42inch bust it is *"difficult go around dressed as a man!"* This reveals a woman confident in her appearance with an ability to make a joke at her own expense.

Margaret features again in a 1969 news report in the *Newcastle Journal*. Continuing with her frequent mention of knowledge of old folklore that was passed down through her family, she tells the reporter of her grandfather, whom I suspect, in this case, is her paternal one:

> *"Her grandfather was a charlatan – her description, not mine – who used to yank teeth out of hypnotised bystanders in market-places and Margaret Bruce, as a youngster, would regularly run off with any raggle-taggle gypsies who happened to pass by her Darlington home ..."*

We also learn that she receives many letters from people asking her for help, such as: *"I am in love with a married man"* and *"I lose £20 a week gambling. Can you make my luck change?"*

The reporter continues:

> *"Miss Bruce claims that, were she that way inclined, she could make a fortune. But her advice to the thwarted lover would be 'lay off' and her counsel to the gambler 'Twenty pounds a week? You're lucky to have it to lose.'*
>
> *She will sell you a love talisman if that's what you want but will write: 'Real love talismans are wedding rings and marriage*

licences.' She will send you the Sachet of Venus ... but suggest that it simply be given, as a present, with a kiss."

The reporter describes an exquisite apothecary of jars, sachets and smells and further comments:

"Here and there, sitting in the way of the nice, neat mail order image is a book on witchcraft – Do you dabble Miss Bruce? – 'I don't.' she says. 'I just know all about it.'"

I can find little solid evidence of Margaret ever having been involved directly in witchcraft or any magical group, though she did have numerous associations with people in magical circles. These included the previously mentioned Madeline Montalban, Nicholas Heron and Gerald Gardner. She also knew Carl Weschcke (Lewellyn Publications); Melita Denning (AKA Vivian Barcynski/Godfrey) of the writing duet Denning and Phillips and past preside of the Order of Bards, Ovates and Druids; as well as Doreen Valiente.

The best, albeit somewhat tenuous, evidence for Margaret having an involvement in witchcraft is seen in Doreen's diaries. At different times, over a period of twenty years, she lists Margaret as someone she thinks attended a ritual at Charles Cardell's property at Charlwood in 1961. Whilst it appears Cardell and Margaret had become business associates in the early 1960s and were reciprocally advertising each other's products in their respective publications, I am inclined to think it unlikely Margaret attended the ritual. Whenever asked by reporters if she is a witch, her reply is always to the negative. Margaret is someone who, as she grew older, increasingly and loudly owned her beliefs, and I have no reason to think that she would have had any qualms about taking ownership of the word 'witch' if she had considered herself such. That said, Charles Cardell would also have never owned up to being a witch or practicing witchcraft, yet I am quite certain he did – but he just didn't call it witchcraft. For historical reasons that were valid for him, he resolutely refused to identify with the word 'witchcraft' and instead referred to his practices as the Old Tradition.

The only thing Margaret does appear to have been "initiated" into is the 31 mysteries of Hinayana Buddhism. This claim is given in the blurb for her Burmese Magick inspired, *Salesman Talisman*. As this was on a sales flyer, it may be due a pinch of salt without the aid of an outside printer.

In the mid 1960s, Margaret established her own printing press under the name Angel Press and produced quite remarkable booklets, seemingly without the aid of an outside printer. In 1964, under the name Margaret Bruce, she produced her first booklet, *A Little Treasury of Love and Magick*. This was followed in 1965 by *The Little Grimoire*. This latter publication used different coloured inks, which was quite advanced tech for those days and some pages show rubricated characters and highlights in various colours. On the back, it states that it was *"designed, written, made, printed and published by Margaret Bruce."*

In the late 60s, Margaret and Gretel moved to Helmington Old Inn (which was by then a house) in Hunwick, County Durham, where Margaret continued her business. At some point in the 60s, she considered buying Aleister Crowley's Boleskine House in Scotland, but found it to be in a state of *"shocking disrepair"*. In the early 70s, they moved into an old, converted railway station at Wolsingham in County Durham. A few years later, they moved to High Rigg House Farm in St John's Chapel, County Durham, where she established the Margaret Bruce Animal Sanctuary, which she ran alongside her mail order business.

For well over 50 years, Margaret created magical wares and produced numerous booklets, pamphlets and leaflets. When she sent you one of her Magickal products, it would be wrapped in strongly scented leaflets promoting her other products, whilst also (ironically) imploring you to consider the environmental impact of paper.

In the 1980s and 90s, there would often be thoughtful stickers added saying things like "Given with love by somebody who truly cares," or "Posted within one hour of receiving your kind letter."

Some of her publications mention her "Golden Jubilee" from 1936 to 1986. She would have been 9 or 10 years-old in 1936, and this ties in with her having a magical awakening at quite a young age, as seen in the previously mentioned account of her by Gardner.

Margaret had a very respectable depth to her occult knowledge and understanding, as seen through numerous incarnations of her mail-order catalogue. When writing descriptions, she often included old wives' tales, things she learnt from her grandmother, some old folklore recipe she "discovered" as well as real magical knowledge. In a 1972 news article with the eye-grabbing heading "Sex-Swap Man Cashes in On Love Potions," she informs us that she is *"Britain's last working folk botanist"* and is patronised by nobility. Her specialist area seems to have been in using herbs and resins to create fragrances and incense and she would seek out old recipes at the British Museum.

Margaret had great skill in making these exquisite perfumes, which included a scent for both men and women, called "Satyr" – made from musk, ambergris and civet, plus *the one un-named and unmentionable ingredient that is essential to its composition."* Margaret was selling "Satyr" for £1 a phial in 1972. By the 1990s, its price had increased to £20, probably due to price rises on the natural resources she was using. She tells us that *"mere mortals who wish to enjoy the divine fragrance of Satyr perfume may do so only while dwindling stocks last."* "Satyr" contains the same ingredients as Crowley's infamous "Ruthvah". Margaret, however, attributes its recipe to her grandfather, Alfred T. Raper, stating that he used to make it to an ancient Arabian formula and that this was copied and renamed "Ruthvah" by Crowley.

Margaret also makes a likely reference to her maternal grandmother, Sarah Myers, who married Alfred Raper. One of Margaret's Pamphlets from 1981 is entitled: *Frankincense, Myrrh and Wild Weardale Magick* by Sarah Myers. Margaret's grandmother had long since passed, but I suspect this is a veiled homage to her and was most likely written by Margaret.

Once she had established her Angel Press imprint, things opened up further for Margaret as it meant she could be in control of nearly everything connected with her business.

Her second Angel Press publication, the 1965 book *The Little Grimoire*, conveys a simplicity that you don't see in her later works. It also has comparatively fewer words per page and more, larger images. Margaret often included illustrations taken from alchemical manuscripts and medieval woodcuts as well as using classic occult symbolism.

Her preface informs us that a grimoire is a small collection of folk spells and recipes, often handed down through generations. After signing her preface with her name, she proudly puts a full-page picture of herself as "Miss Margaret Bruce" immediately afterwards. You are then led on through a meandering mixture of prayers, magical correspondences, astrology, herbs and essences. You find out how to make a "Lavender Suffumigation" and "Love Smoke", do "Butterfly Magick" and create a herbal wine called "Witches' Delight". One of Margaret's hobby horses – "bogus occultism" and "charlatans" – also rears its head and was something that turned into a veritable Padstow Snapper over the forthcoming years.

Nearly twenty years later, her 1984 booklet, *Magick*, suggests she had acquired a different type of typewriter by this point. The typesetting is much better, more modern looking and she uses visually appealing multi-coloured pages. It seems to be one of her longer publications, running at just over 60 pages. This "little book" took her two years to write. The cover is boldly emblazoned with:

"Margaret Bruce's coveted collection of Tried, Proven and Practical Natural, Goetic, Theurgic, Transcendental and Illusory MAGICK as inherited, professed and practiced through seven generations from the year of Our Lord 1777 to the present day."

The preface includes quite a long and scathing warning about *"Flim-Flam"*, *"self-styled adepts"* and *"razzle-dazzle operators"* whom she says have but one skill of *"… turning your money into their money."* Her hobby horse has now fully matured and is given full rein. Her mentions of bogus occultism and derogatory references to charlatans are frequently seen throughout this book. She had reason to believe that others had been copying her products and she shows an ever-growing disdain of fakes offering magic. This, combined with her long-standing belief that Magick cannot be bought, seems to have made her even more outspoken and fervent on this matter.

With her rant over, the preface then continues with the wonderful paragraph:

"This is not simply a book of Magick, but a Magick book. The pages are unlimited by numbers and the Magick dwells in the pauses between the reading of each word and the tuning of the page. Just as music is mere noise without the measured periods of nothing between the notes and chords, so the art and craft of Magick comprises the placing of apparent nothingness in dynamic relationship with apparent realities in order to create a desired result. In order to do this, it is necessary to learn the difference between illusion and reality – a task which may be attempted by perhaps one suitable person in a million. Of a million such aspirants, one partial success might be an optimistic estimate. The ability of the reader to comprehend this basic fact is all that limits the Magick of this book."

In 1990, Margaret officially retired whilst in her mid-60's but continued with her mail order business and tending to her organic farm. By the early 1990s, she stopped advertising her Magickal wares but seems to have retained a connection with her loyal customer base whilst selling off the final bits from her now dwindling stock. She comments on how her now arthritic fingers prevent her from making more than a few copper talismans per year but she will endeavour to do so for those who desire one.

She informs us on how changes in the law prevent her from ever being able to make some of her scents again. I suspect this is due to the difficulties in obtaining raw materials such as ambergris, a natural by-product produced by the sperm whale. It does not require the killing of a whale but has been difficult to obtain for some years due to it now being a protected species. Rare lumps of ambergris are occasionally found on UK beaches and are still considered fair game. Her scents that fell foul of these legislative changes included Satyr, Ruggiero and Aphrodite Water and she poignantly tells us they will *"now be no more than memories."*

Margaret also mentions how she still has two hand-forged Athame blanks and an incised Key of Solomon Hazel, as commissioned by Gerald Gardner in the 1950s, and says that they are reminders of how folklore has been superseded by *"New Ageism"* in four decades.

In the final few years of her life, she started writing newsletters that she would send out to her remaining clients. They are full of stories about the nature she sees around her, the animals on her farm, and the difficulties with keeping up with the challenges bought about with the changing faces of the seasons.

For over twenty years, she planted trees and did conservational work at High Rigg House Farm whilst becoming largely self-sufficient; living on the edible produce brought to her by her various animals, which included geese and hens. She mourns the loss of days gone by, when neighbours would drop by to barter milk, eggs, cheese and home-baked bread – commenting on how she now just glimpses *"aloof strangers speeding past in their shiny motor cars."*

Her anti-media and press stance, as usual, takes up significant passages of the newsletters – as too does her continuing issue with those she considers fakes. Long comments are made about the decay of governments and society around her and the environmental catastrophes she firmly believes imminent. She talks of how irksome it is dealing with those who try to coerce her *"into using dangerous chemicals and barbaric farming practices, under threat of draconian penalties for non-compliance."*

I want to end with some words from Margaret: *"All sanity, all reality, all nature is, together with Magick, retreating from the suffocating menace of mankind. If you wish to discover real Magick, perhaps you should hurry!"*

Thoughts on Being Called a Heretic

CHATTERING MAGPIE

During a recent so-called 'private discussion' on a Facebook wall (where, in truth, nothing, absolutely nothing is private) belonging to a Roman Catholic friend of mine, a complete stranger to me (but obviously a Roman Catholic friend of my said friend) called me a Pagan; and one other (an Anglican) a heretic.

I will not bore the reader with the details, as in point of fact they have, and the discussion itself had no real bearing upon the context of the usage of 'heretic'. Rather, I wish to emphasise that outside of history books and humour, this word is not generally heard in my circles. Certainly, it is not used publicly within Interfaith by Roman Catholics of my acquaintance, which is in itself a consolation.

A heretic is said to be one who's opinion or views are held to be contrary to the accepted teachings of the group to which they (may) belong. For heresy to be held theoretically valid as an accusation, both the accuser and the accused should be members of that same group.

For example, the online dictionary known as *Wiktionary* lists the noun 'heretic' as: "someone who in the opinion of others believes contrary to the fundamental tenets of a religion he claims to belong to." Many other dictionaries, both physical and online, share a similar opinion.

There are words, terminologies and phases that when used may tell us more about the user than the person being described.

For example, it is said that Winston Churchill once described the great Mahatma Ghandi as "a half naked Indian fakir."

The first part of this statement is perfectly true, the Mahatma habitually wore only a cotton sheet and nothing more, and he was quite obviously Indian. However, the use of the word 'fakir' is here meant as a derogatory and disingenuous insult to describe a street entertainer or cheap conjuror. It is certainly not meant in a respectful manner to describe a Hindu holy man. The phase "a half naked Indian fakir" does no particular harm to the reputation of the Mahatma, but instead reflects badly on the reputation of the man who would later become Britain's wartime Prime Minister.

Men and women are a reflection of their time, in the sense that they reflect the society in which they live. The statement made by Churchill strengthens our opinion of him as an imperialist and, quite probably, as that of a racist. It also suggests that at the time, others would have shared his opinion. His statement is a political one that is deliberately designed to appeal to others of a similar and now outdated opinion.

Technically, from an historical perspective, a Roman Catholic calling an Anglican a heretic could be deemed correct. The Anglican Church is part of that greater Protestant Movement, whose origins obviously lie with the Reformation and the ultimate break with the Church of Rome. From the perspective of a Roman Catholic therefore, a member of the Protestant Churches does hold opinions contrary to the accepted teachings of the group (Christianity) to which they both (in theory) belong. It is perhaps only fair to point out that, again, from this historical perspective, a Protestant could call a Roman Catholic a heretic, as both believe that they represent the 'correct' way.

By this same argument, calling a Pagan a heretic is plain wrong. A Pagan does not belong to the same group, nor does a Pagan accept the same teachings. However, these are technicalities. The question really is should such words as 'heretic' be used or be accepted in the modern era? Are not such words as 'heretic', or even 'infidel', barriers to Interfaith and are they not an indication that some elements within our society are closed to concepts of inclusivity and pluralism?

It was certainly an educational experience for me to discover that there are some Roman Catholics who are as fundamentalist and closed to alternative perspectives as the more usual so-called 'Christian Fundie' that is portrayed in the media. Like all fundamentalists, they are, one assumes, a member of the insecure minority. However, this situation may also illustrate something that I have commented on before – that in Interfaith, we are in a sense really preaching to the converted, as only the most open-minded, spiritually secure and forward-thinking are often prepared to engage in such dialogue.

The question remains however, how do we reach out and educate those individuals whose minds are so closed and whose distrust of other's faiths is such that they genuinely believe the use of the word 'heretic' to be acceptable behaviour? That, unfortunately, is a question that remains unanswered and, in a sense, reflects the complexity of the Interfaith Movement.

Perhaps it is time that the actual practice of engagement, as opposed to the principle, was discussed more openly within the Pagan Movement, recognising that the Pagan Movement demands and expects equality.

Universal Fire Circle Alchemy

JEFF MAGNUS MCBRIDE AND
ABIGAIL SPINNER MCBRIDE

At the fire circle, as in life, we each carry around our own
quandaries and calamities, material which often nurtures
impediments or "blocks" that perpetuate unsavoury patterns
of stagnation. These internal obstructions can be visualized as
literal blocks of salt, a substance that is not only alchemically
symbolic, but also long-recognised. This being said, on a more
cerebral level, salt can be linked to the preservation of memories;
while, on the affective plain it is appropriately associated to
the preservation of feelings. These languished memories and
feelings, whether we are conscious of them or not, become a
platform for the emergence, reappearance, recurrence and re-
enactment of dramas with analogous mythopoetic foundations.
Thus, salt is in fact a metonymy for that which sustains us in futile
and ineffective cognitive and behaviour processes.

Enveloped in the pervasive intensity of the alchemical vessel,
immersed in the inter-activity of drum, dance, and creative
play, absorbed in the profundity of trance, blocks get stimulated
and dislodged organically. When a particular threshold is
attained, the sulphur, or energetic heat released by the Fire,
together with the fervour of drumming and movement, triggers
a symbolic liquefaction of the salt within. This natural element
of the alchemical progression is embodied through perspiration
and tears, a corporeal expression of the mental and spiritual
liberation it signifies. The emotional overflowing and experience

of soul-stirring sensation that accompanies this literal brimming over of the personal vessel has consistently been referred to as "popping" but we render a perpetual distinction by considering it more incisively, as a release, which leads to real ease. Real ease in life is what truly empowers our connections to Spirit, to ourselves, and each other to flourish and thrive.

By accepting the challenge of navigating through these processes and committing to the ordeal, we are inherently provided with the blueprint for illumination in the truest sense … not guru-sitting-on-a-pillow illuminated, but shedding-new-light-on-our-lives illuminated.

The Fire Circle is a microcosm for the macrocosm of our aggregate existence, and, therefore, any core issue or challenge we encounter in our daily life will ineluctably be activated and echoed within the vessel. As we encounter and sometimes collide with these issues, it is our ability to negotiate the situation inside the Circle, while remaining engaged in the process, which affords us the prospect and probability of returning to a daily life where these matters no longer activate us. The magic we co-create in the sacred container, through sustained engagement, ripples out exponentially into the rest of our lives, for the highest good. The mightier our ability to remain engaged in the Fire Circle process, the richer and fuller our experience becomes – a truth that is mirrored in the greater mystery of life. Though it can be challenging to stay fully committed to the creative process from midnight, or earlier, until after sunrise, it is specifically this kind of initiatory, inventive ordeal, virtually unheard of in our culture, that furnishes us with the utmost opportunity for personal and collective growth.

WORKING WITH PRIMA MATERIA

When issues come up, friends often say, "What's the matter?" So, let us examine the "first matter" or Prima Materia of alchemy, which is referred to interchangeably in alchemical texts and literature as: darkness, chaos, excrement or lead. It is precisely this material (which many of us speciously dismiss as useless, insignificant, bothersome, and even infuriating) from whence the final golden product is derived. To transform lead into gold, or to spiritualize matter; alchemists, and likewise, we at the Fire, utilize the following formula: "Solve et Coagula", or "dissolve and recombine".

The initiation into the Great Work of Alchemy involves first the application of heat, and subsequently the addition of water to catalyze the dissolving, melting, and liquefying of the first matter. In his alchemical writings, Carl Jung characterized this period as *"breaking down the boundaries of the ego, and allowing the chaotic material of the unconscious to pour forth where it can be inspected by consciousness."* In this sense, the alchemical expression, "Solve", quite accurately describes the initial interactions with self and others that take place in the early hours of the Fire Circle – interactions that reflect the softening of personal and group boundaries, and the opening of hearts.

The second half of the alchemical idiom guiding the Fire Circle ritual is "Coagula", literally "coagulate" – an expression that denotes a re-assimilation with self, others, and refined understanding. In terms of the alchemical process, this is the reunification that occurs after the purifying stage of distillation. In life, we can observe this corollary of the Work through our integration of the lessons and experiences we have had around the fire into our community relations and through our ability to further assimilate them into the orbit of our daily lives, in our much grander circle around the fire of the sun.

THE ALCHEMICAL PROCESS

During the course of an all-night fire, as well as a Fire Circle succession, time periods with distinct energetic signatures are clearly discernable; three comprehensive periods, along with their constituent components, are alchemically referenced as follows:

Nigredo:

The Latin term for the first phase of the alchemical process is Nigredo, meaning "the blackening". In the laboratory, this is the phase where the "Prima Materia", or first matter, is placed into a container and burned to ash, then dissolved to produce a suspension. Within the Fire Circle, Nigredo is evidenced as a vast expanse of chaotic, often frenetic activity – from the arrival and acclimation of celebrants, to the excitement of the Fire-lighting ceremony, to highly energized drumming and dancing. On a personal or transformational level, this is a time when we "burn away and dissolve" whatever stands between us and the Divine. The three stages of alchemy encompassed by the Nigredo phase are:

1. Calcination (root chakra, Saturn, survival): The issue or issues within the physical container are brought up and heated by the Fire of chanting, drumming, dancing, and other creative expression.
2. Dissolution (sacral chakra, Jupiter, blending): The issues are dissolved in the sea of personal and collective emotion. Through sweat and tears, salt is released from the physical body, as blocks begin to dissolve.
3. Separation (solar plexus chakra, Mars, choosing): In the alchemist's laboratory, this is the stage when the solution is broken up into its separate components. At the Fire Circle, people begin to sacrifice whatever Lead they've been carrying into the fire to be transformed. A choice is made to separate or release from the "issue" (energetic discharge, more tears, or intense physical movement), and in so doing separate from

the things which isolate our individual egos from others and Self.

Albedo:

The Albedo phase, which in more orthodox alchemy relates to the whitening process, is a time when the matter in the flask is softening and beginning to purify. Translated to the vernacular of the Fire Circle, this phase corresponds to a palpable lightening of the energy; perhaps the drumming grows quieter, or the songs and chants move to a place of more richness and depth, or the dancing becomes increasingly lyrical. Coincidentally, this is often the time when the sky begins to grow light. The above and the below are united in the heart, resulting in a vibration of increased purity and strength. The three stages of the alchemical process that comprise the Albedo phase are:

4. Conjunction (heart chakra, Venus, joining together through love): The shift to Albedo, the white, soft stage of the Work. This step represents the coming together of Self and ego, soul and spirit, or the individual and the community. An important step; often it gives us a deeper understanding of our Higher Self in contrast to our ego. At the Fire Circle, deeper connections are forged between the person releasing and the other celebrants who witness, receive or catch the energy and assist gently through the process.
5. Fermentation (throat chakra, Mercury, speaking): In Alchemy, fermentation is the process of refining, skimming the crud that rises to the surface, to find a purer solution. We have had the experience of burning, dissolving, separating, and joining together. Now, we are speaking our truth and separating the subtle from the gross as we continue to refine.
6. Distillation (third eye chakra, Moon, introspective visioning): At this stage of the Work, we have a pure, refined "solution".

We gain insight and understanding by "processing" our issues through the alchemical laboratory that is our body. By contemplating the past, while being engaged in the present, we can now make informed choices about how to move and interact at the Fire, and out in the world in the future.

Rubedo:

The culminating phase of the alchemical process is called "Rubedo", meaning "the reddening" – an expression which, within the confines of a conventional laboratory, indicates the material's conversion to a red tint, and presages its transformation to gold. In the tradition of Fire Circle Alchemy, this can be equated with the sunrise itself. Of this mystery, few words can be said. The stage that corresponds with the Rubedo is:

7. Coagulation (crown chakra, Sun, illuminating): This begins the phase of Rubedo, the period in which our spiritual gold is realized. This is the stage of consciously connecting with Spirit, releasing the light within matter, and releasing the boundaries between inner and outer experience. We bring our fresh insights and knowledge into the world, moment by moment, remaining in the flow. We connect with our highest selves, connect with Divinity, and with the Earth. Also at this stage, we experience an accelerated rate of synchronicities.

At this point in the alchemical work, we re-enter the fire of our daily lives, with our hearts connected, and our minds set free. As we continue the practice in the circle of life, new issues will inevitably arise within us, and the refining process will begin again.

Both the physical laboratory of the alchemist and the virtual laboratory of the Fire Circle are very much like the laboratory of the body. Each is in a perpetual state of evolution: processing blocks, pushing boundaries, and, as the Hermetica states, *"separating the subtle from the gross, gently and with great ingenuity."*

Fire Circle Alchemy is not inevitably bound by temporal or spatial constraints. This is not to say that an Alchemical Fire Circle ritual is by no means obliged to persist until dawn, nor is it requisite that it manifest outdoors. A group of three or more friends gathered together with common intent can converge upon this application for a period of a few hours to generate a genuinely magical experience. In contrast, this ritual format has also proven exceedingly effective for groups of several hundred; drumming, singing and dancing all night long, until sunrise and beyond. We encourage you to experiment, for you are the alchemists!

Who Will Plow my Vulva? – Inanna as an Insatiable Goddess of Love

MELISSA SEIMS

When we hear the name Inanna, the story of her mystical descent through the seven gates, deep into the Underworld is the one aspect of her tale that tends to most readily spring to mind. Probably because it resonates with our own experiences of periods of blackness, and I suspect that there are few people who cannot relate in some way to it. The trials and anguishes caused by states of despair, when life has gone distinctly pear-shaped and all around seems to be veiled in darkness as you blindly claw your way through internal, twisty, dark tunnels with a desperation to find the light of understanding, lest you should lose the path for good. Finally, there is (hopefully) a symbolic rebirth, a re-emergence, and you find yourself older, wiser and with a few more wrinkles.

My understanding of Inanna changed when I came across the book, *Inanna Queen of Heaven and Earth – Her Stories and Hymns from Sumer*, by Diane Wolkstein and Samuel Noah Kramer. I was immediately struck by the image of Inanna on the front, which appeared to depict a smiling, crowned Goddess with long plaits and what look like phalluses protruding from her shoulders; we are told that these are actually feathers! I realised that there was much more to Inanna than what is commonly thought or indeed, portrayed – for Inanna's descent is only a very small part of her epic story.

Wolkstein and Kramer's book is essentially a translation of the inscriptions of the Inanna myth found on ancient Sumerian stone tablets that were unearthed from amongst the ruins of Nippur, one of the most ancient cities of Babylonia and the cultural and spiritual centre for Sumer, which nowadays corresponds to the region of Southern Iraq. The tablets are thought to date from around 1750 B.C. and were excavated by the University of Pennsylvania between 1889 and 1900. Samuel Kramer was a key figure in piecing together and translating the texts found on the broken tablets, whilst Diane Wolkstein, a folklorist and storyteller, took the time to study the language, culture and history of ancient Sumer and presents us with her inspired interpretation of Inanna's myth, based on the translated texts.

Upon opening the book, you will discover the delightful tale of Inanna as "a young woman who loved to laugh," who plucks and then lovingly cares for the Huluppu tree. Thought by some to refer to a willow, poplar or a date palm, it also has some obvious parallels with the Tree of Life.

To Inanna's dismay, a serpent makes its nest in the Huluppu, as too does the fearsome lion-headed Anzu bird and that "demon" of unbridled sexuality, Lilith. This imagery is said to represent Inanna's unexpressed fears and desires and gives her character a maiden-like quality.

After much weeping (adolescent angst?), Inanna's brother Gilgamesh comes and chops down the tree with his big and shiny axe, an action that seems to symbolise the end of her childhood. From the wood is made a throne and more importantly, a bed; for Inanna is now ready to become a woman and a queen.

Inanna then embarks on an epic journey, through which she comes to be mentally, spiritually and emotionally fertilised by a meeting with her (grand) father Enki, who is both the God of

Wisdom and the God of Water – a vital component of fertility when it comes to vegetation and growth. In ancient Sumerian, the word for water is synonymous with the word for semen. When Inanna reaches Enki's temple at Eridu, "where kingship descended from heaven," they sit up all night getting drunk and in his inebriated state, Enki offers Inanna all manner of gifts, many of which are conceptual (these are the Me, the gifts of civilisation). Upon receiving the gift of decision-making, she decides to take all the Me for herself and for her people. Loading them onto her "Boat of Heaven", she beats a hasty retreat before Enki can change his mind.

Enki awakens to sobriety and realising what he has done, creates various magical monsters and sends them off after Inanna. Altogether, there are seven attempts by Enki to prevent his daughter from getting home with the divine Me. These seem to be analogous to the seven challenges Inanna later faces at the seven gates leading down to the Underworld domain of Queen Ereshkigal, who in some versions of this myth is identified as being Enki's twin sister. In this instance, however, Enki's sorcery is trying to stop Inanna's return from the realm of the gods, back to her home city of Uruk. He is foiled every time by Ninshubar (who appears to represent Inanna's higher self), and so the goddess returns safely from Eridu with the heavenly Me and, along with them, her own sovereignty.

Inanna's throne is now befitting of her, but her special bed is still empty. After more wiliness (male, this time), she finally falls for Dumuzi (also called Tammuz), a vegetation god who is also a mortal shepherd (bear in mind here that in Sumer, a sheepfold was often used as a metaphor for female genitalia).

This section of Wolkstein's translation, with its obvious and abundant sexual metaphors, makes for erotic reading as we find Inanna declaring:

"My vulva, the horn,
The Boat of Heaven,
Is full of eagerness like the young moon.
My untilled land lies fallow.
As for me, Inanna,
Who will plow my vulva?
Who will plow my high field?
Who will plow my wet ground?"

Dumuzi courteously replies that he would be more than happy to plow Inannas vulva for *"At the king's lap stood the rising cedar."* Inanna then sings:

"He has sprouted; he has burgeoned;
He is lettuce planted by the water
He is the one my womb loves best [...]
My honey-man, my honey-man sweetens me always.
My lord, the honey-man of the gods,
He is the one my womb loves best.
His hand is honey, his foot is honey,
He sweetens me always [...]
Make your milk sweet and thick, my bridegroom.
My shepherd, I will drink your fresh milk.
Wild bull, Dumuzi, make your milk sweet and thick.
I will drink your fresh milk.
Let the milk of the goat flow in my sheepfold.
Fill my holy churn with honey cheese.
Lord Dumuzi, I will drink your fresh milk."

According to modern Sumerian theologians and mythographers, these Sumerian love songs were integral to Inanna's status as a love goddess, but not of the modern 'sweetness and light' kind, for Inanna was also very ambitious and aggressive. The 'darker' (not to be construed negatively) aspects of Inanna as a goddess

190

of love can be seen in the Goddess Ereshkigal, who rules over the Underworld and torments Inanna during her descent, for Ereshkigal is also Inanna's older, darker, sister, nemesis and shadow self. The side Inanna must face before she can truly return and take control of not only her kingdom, but her whole being. For without the darkness, we would not be able to distinguish the light; and without knowing both, we wouldn't know the place of balance which sits in-between.

So, Inanna descends and confronts her dark side, Ereshkigal, who, with her equally raging, yet more devouring and compulsive sexuality, seems to demand only her own self-satisfaction. Having stripped Inanna of everything, she slings her on a meat hook and leaves her to die. However, Inanna's spiritual self, Ninshubur, as previously instructed by Inanna, appeals to the gods, and through Enki's intervention, Inanna is reborn in the Underworld. A passageway that links the Great Above (light) to the Great Below (dark) is created, through which Inanna is allowed to leave. But, there is a price to pay, for *"No one ascends from the underworld unmarked ... She must provide someone in her place ..."* Inanna returns to the Great Above and finds that her lover Dumuzi has let power go to his head during her absence. So, Inanna sends him off to the Underworld to face his darker side and to take her place. Fortunately, the 'lighter' side of Inanna (perhaps realising that she would be barren without him) allows his return and resurrection every six months; at which point his sister, Geshtinanna, takes his place. In Sumer, this annual rebirth of Dumuzi and his subsequent marriage to Inanna was celebrated every year at the spring equinox in the sacred marriage ritual (the hieros gamos).

This part of Inanna's story appears to share something in common with that of Hades and Persephone. Whilst Hades is now commonly portrayed as the bad guy, he was also known by the Greeks as 'The Wealthy One' and was often pictured with an overflowing cornucopia. Similarly, in some versions of the myth, it was actually Persephone who was the 'destroyer' and the Queen of the Underworld, with the Orphic mystics celebrating her as the Goddess of the Blessed Dead.

The changing status of many an old god and goddess can be seen elsewhere. For example, in the story of Aphrodite – a goddess who seems to be heralded these days as the Goddess of Love, and who is depicted in TV shows such as 'Xena' as a ditzy, ringlet-encrusted blonde. However, if one digs about a bit you also find fragmentary stories identifying her with Epitymbia, 'on the graves'; and Androphonos, 'man-killer'. These aspects could be seen as a manifestation of Aphrodite's rulership over the Underworld as also suggested by both Persephone's and Inanna's stories – plus, it gives you that powerful link between sex and death.

Over time, perspectives change due to political and historical events, resulting in the distortion of many a myth. The last two thousand years, with its strong, patriarchal, Christian influences, have meant that sacred prostitutes and extrovert, sexual love goddesses have been downplayed or even demonised and modern depictions of goddesses of love seem to come nicely packaged, complete with glitter, and largely devoid of wanton, rampant sexuality. It's not just goddesses either. On a trip to Rome I was struck by the fact that so many of the beautiful statues of Pan, Dionysus and Bacchus have at some point in the past had their genitals chipped off lest they offend. Can you imagine it – Pan without a prick!

How often do you see a love goddess depicted with wreaths of flowers, with an enchantingly smiley face and maybe a cupid with an arrow, above her shoulder? Now think, how many of these kitsch love goddesses are depicted in an obvious state of full-on, in-your-face, sexual rapture? If you pick up some of the mainstream modern books on love magic, you can guarantee that Aphrodite will be in there (minus the sitting on graves reference), but what of Inanna with her broad-spectrum sexuality and her vulva that was *"wondrous to behold"*? If you do a search for love goddesses on Ebay, you will be faced with pages and pages of very nice, voluptuous goddesses bedecked with stars, butterflies and flowers. Lewd, maniacally grinning Sheela-na-gigs or overtly sexual goddesses with legs fiercely and passionately parted are a relatively rare find.

Inanna's story not only celebrates her as a love goddess, for if you accept that Ereshkigal is Inanna's shadow self, her myth also celebrates her sexuality in both its nurturing and devouring aspects (for the latter, Crowley's *Leah Sublime* springs to mind). Inanna's myth also reminds us that sex and love are not divorced from each other, for during her passionate courtship with Dumuzi, we are told *"Sweet is the sleep of hand-to-hand. Sweeter still the sleep of heart-to-heart"* and she refers to Dumuzi as *"My sweet love, lying by my heart."* It is this compassionate aspect of her being that welcomes his return from the Underworld every six months.

Whilst modern society seems capable of separating sex and love, one can't help but wonder if this is just encouraging a hedonistic, self-centredness that divorces the heart from the soul; a path 32 period, or perhaps we should call it the 'path of self-service.' I can't help but feel that this is a bit like Inanna leaving Dumuzi in the Underworld with her darker sister/self, Queen Ereshkigal, for good. How then would the Queen of Heaven and Earth be fertilised?

I have merely touched upon Inanna's epic, complex and multi-layered story which seems to take us from the heights of spiritual inspiration, down to the darker recesses of our mind. Like a good tarot deck, you can interpret a good myth in multiple ways and use its messages to reflect on your own sense of self. So, if you fancy a good read and have had your interest aroused (pun intended) by the small extracts given herein, get yourself a copy of this book – you probably won't think of Inanna in quite the same way again.

ALSO BY MARION PEARCE

The Roman Calendar: Origins and Festivals, published by Fenix Flames of Nottingham. This book explores the origins of our calendar which dates back to ancient Rome. The festivals are described, from the wild excesses of the Lupercalia to the gentler pastoral Floralia and Ambarvalia, the Roman zest for life shines through their year.

Celtic Sacrifice: Pre-Christian Ritual and Religion, published by Fenix Flames of Nottingham. Combining sources from mythology and archaeology with eye witness accounts from the period, this book presents a fascinating picture of Celtic religion and worship and diety.

The Gods of the Vikings published by Avalonia. Illustrated by Emily Carding. The Norse Gods are as vivid and powerful as the rugged elemental landscape they ruled over. The influence of the Norse and Saxon gods are considered further through their survival in British customs and significant calendar Festivals.

Milton Keynes UK
Ingram Content Group UK Ltd.
UKHW022252020524
442136UK00010B/361

9 781915 580184